Monica Pitek-Fugedi is a mental health therapist specializing in anxiety and trauma. Monica is the owner of Whole Mind Wellness, PLLC, where she sees people in person and virtually across the state of Michigan. Monica has written two e-books about managing anxiety, hosts the Whole Mind Wellness Podcast, and writes a blog on her website www.wholemindwellnesspllc.com.

You can watch Monica's Tedx Talk by visiting the Whole Mind Wellness PLLC YouTube Page.

Monica lives in West Bloomfield Twp, Michigan with her husband, son and dog.

Follow Monica on Facebook (Whole Mind Wellness), Instagram and YouTube.

This book is dedicated to anyone who has ever or is currently experiencing cancer, and those who love them.

Monica Pitek-Fugedi

SHADE OF PINK

AUSTIN MACAULEY PUBLISHERS™

LONDON • CAMBRIDGE • NEW YORK • SHARJAH

Ordering Information
Quantity sales: Special discounts are available on quantity purchases by corporations, associations, and others. For details, contact the publisher at the address below.

Publisher's Cataloging-in-Publication data
Pitek-Fugedi, Monica
Shade of Pink

ISBN 9781649790965 (Paperback)
ISBN 9781649790972 (ePub e-book)

Library of Congress Control Number: 2021925312

www.austinmacauley.com/us

First Published 2022
Austin Macauley Publishers LLC
40 Wall Street, 33rd Floor, Suite 3302
New York, NY 10005
USA

mail-usa@austinmacauley.com
+1 (646) 5125767

Preface

I'm not a fan of doctors. Seems like every time I go when I think I am sick, they tell me I am not sick, so I just end up not going. This usually means when I really am sick, it tends to get worse before it gets better. For instance, I didn't see a doctor until I had strep throat so bad that I couldn't open my mouth. I didn't go see someone until the abscess in my throat became so severe, I was sleeping 36 hours straight and unable to eat. The doctor sent me to the emergency room where I was told I could have died if I waited much longer.

When I discovered a lump in my breast, going to the doctor seemed like more of an annoyance than anything. I'm pretty cystic, so I just figured that they would tell me to stop drinking coffee or something. But then it seemed to be getting a little bigger.

While having a wine night with a group of friends, somehow we got on the subject of boobs, which is not uncommon for wine nights. Our topics usually cover things much more extensive than that. I casually mentioned that I had a lump in my right breast about the size of a golf ball. The ladies encouraged me to go to the doctor. Then when I didn't, they encouraged me some more. I told a few other close friends about this, and they also not so gently encouraged me to go to a doctor. One of my friends, who also happens to be my coworker, came into my office, shut the door, and wouldn't leave until I called for an appointment.

I credit these women in my life for saving my life. Without their annoying nudges, I may have never made an appointment. I was stage 2 by the time I went to see someone. I could have gotten to stage 4 and been looking at a far more daunting future than I am looking at now. Friends are important for so many reasons. Wine is important for so many reasons. Together, they save lives.

Introduction

The scariest thing I've ever done was willingly jump out of an airplane from 3,000 feet in the air. And when I say I jumped out of an airplane, I mean I… just me, jumped out of an airplane. No tandem, just me and the air, hoping I paid close enough attention to know where the parachute chord was. I would like to say I did this because I am a risk-taker who likes to face my fears head-on and challenge myself to do new things. But the reality is, I did it to impress a boy.

As I stood on the platform of the plane, peering down at the miniature houses, I started to wonder if this guy was really worth all this. When you jump out of an airplane, you are supposed to count to ten before you open your chute. There is nothing quite as scary as plummeting toward the ground at top speed. The whole time, my hand clung to the string for dear life. If this didn't go well, I could die. And I knew FOR SURE this boy was not worth dying over.

I never counted to ten so fast in my life. I pulled the string, my chute opened, and I was yanked back up in the air before my speed declined. I found myself gliding effortlessly toward the earth. My anxiety turned to peace as I took the time to admire a bird's eye view of the land below.

The exhilaration I felt as I landed was incomparable to anything I have ever experienced. I did this. I jumped out of a plane. The reason is not as important as the fact that I did it. Had I allowed myself to give in to my fear, I would have never known the excitement that comes with taking a risk. I would have stayed in my comfort zone and missed out on a really cool experience. But you know what they say about comfort zones: they are beautiful places, but nothing ever grows there.

Up until the spring of 2017, jumping out of an airplane was the scariest thing I had ever done. I had stupidly thought if I could jump out of an airplane, I could do anything. And then May 9, 2017 happened. I remember it clearly because that is the day that I died.

Let me back up a little and tell you a little bit about how I lived. From a very young age, maybe three or four, I remember being called cute. When I was little, I had long, golden blonde hair. I used to make my mom put curlers in it every night so that I would wake up to beautiful waves. My mom never gave me the message that my hair made me cute, but society did, and the message never stopped. As I got older, 'cute' turned into 'pretty'. I used pretty as a label to define myself. My appearance was the armor I hid behind. It helped me mask my fear of getting found out— found out I wasn't smart enough, wasn't good enough, or wasn't funny enough.

I lived with imposter syndrome. You know, when you feel like people are eventually going to find out you have nothing to offer. I hid behind my appearance, afraid to show the world who I really was for fear that it wouldn't be good enough.

My hair was hands down my finest accessory. It was something to be admired: easy to manage, easy to style, constantly complimented. It was the shield I could hide behind so I didn't have to be vulnerable. It framed my face and gave people the illusion of beauty. No one needed to know who I really was. I was the tall, thin, pretty blonde. I didn't have to be anything else. I didn't know if I could be anyone else. It was comfortable. Never in a million years did I think my whole identity, my whole world, would come crashing down in one short phone call.

Chapter 1

When Intuition Speaks, Trust That Bitch

I found a lump in my breast in October of 2016. It felt like a small golf ball. My intuition told me something was awry, but my mind tried to convince me otherwise. I kept trying to forget about it, thinking if I didn't acknowledge it, then it was not there. Bad logic, I know. I began telling my friends about it. In hindsight, I realize I did this to create accountability for myself. I knew the friends I chose to tell would keep bugging me until I made an appointment for a mammogram.

When I finally did, I can't say I was totally surprised when the results came back concerning. They insisted I get the lump biopsied just to be sure. I might add, at 42, this was my first mammogram. I switched doctors because I moved and my previous doctor said women without a history don't have to have a mammogram until they're 50. If I had waited until I was 50, I would be dead. I am sure of this. What my previous doctor did not take into account is that breast cancer does not reserve itself for those who have a history of cancer. He also did not take into account that I had years of infertility treatments.

In a span of three years, I had three IUIs (intrauterine inseminations) and six in vitro treatments. Not to mention the Clomid and other oral fertility medications I was on before that. I vaguely remember my infertility specialist telling me that this treatment increases my risk of breast cancer. But, like any woman who wants to be a mom, I didn't care. Honestly, I still don't. I wouldn't change my decision to try to conceive. I ultimately ended up adopting, but that is a story for another book.

Three days after my biopsy, my husband and I traveled to Chicago with our eight-year-old son to celebrate our wedding anniversary. I kept getting a nudging feeling all weekend that something was wrong. It would come in waves, and I would shake it off, trying not to think about it. The weekend was beautiful. Clear skies and low 70s. There was a Polish festival going on, which was extra exciting since we are all Polish. We went to the hands-on museum, the big bean, and walked all around Chicago. It was a fabulous weekend.

When I returned to work on Monday, May 8, 2017, it was business as usual. I worked as a high school counselor in a suburb of Detroit. I got to work, turned on my computer, got a cup of coffee, and a few students waiting to ask questions greeted me. A typical day. At 8:00 AM my office phone rang. I usually don't pick up my phone at work. I let it go to voicemail so I can listen to what the problem is before I call back. I don't like being caught off guard. But for some reason, this time I picked up. There's that intuition again. It was my doctor on the other end calling me with the results of my biopsy. She said she wanted me to come in at

11 AM, and she didn't like to have these conversations over the phone. Two things are wrong with that.

One, SHE doesn't like to have these conversations over the phone. I was perfectly happy to have that conversation over the phone. Secondly, she told me the news by not telling me the news; if it was good news, she either wouldn't be telling me at all, or she wouldn't say that she didn't want to tell me until she saw me in person. In any case, I forced it out of her. Cancer, she said. I have cancer. She told me she thought it was stage 1, and that it was highly treatable. She wouldn't stop talking. I finally stopped her and said that I am sure everything she is saying is very important, but I stopped listening after the word *cancer*.

Such an emotionally charged word. It's like a three-ton brick being thrown at you. It's like a tsunami forming with its sole goal to envelop you in its waves. Although my intuition told me something was up, it didn't alleviate the shock I had when I heard that word. When you hear you have cancer, most of us immediately think of death. The doctor kept telling me that I was going to be fine, but all I could think was, *What if I'm not?*

When I got off the phone, I immediately called my husband, Joe. He answered with his usual upbeat demeanor. Through my tears, I told him I had cancer. He was in shock and kept spouting off questions, none of which I had answers for. I told him I would meet him at home at 10:30. When I get bad news, my modus operandi is to go straight in denial. For this reason, I am often pretty level-headed during crises. It takes a while for reality to catch up with me. This time was a little different, but it didn't occur to me that I should leave work at 8 AM when I didn't have to be at the doctor until 11:00. What would I do in that three hours but cry?

So I decided to stay at work. The one person who was in her office after I spoke with my husband was my coworker, Karen. I don't think she realizes how important she was at that moment. She was the first person I told after my husband. Her reaction was perfect. She listened to me, cried, and then said, "Well, now you have a built-in reason to be a bitch." This made me laugh, which was exactly what I needed. I can't imagine the awkwardness and helplessness she felt as I put her into such an awkward and helpless position.

I didn't want to tell anyone else before I told my closest work friend, and honestly, one of my closest real-life friends, Lezah. She was one of those important women in my life who kept hounding me to make an appointment for a mammogram. When I went into her office, she shut the door and hugged me. I didn't say a word, but she just knew. She told me it was going to be okay. All of this happened before she knew the diagnosis. Talk about intuition. I cried on her shoulder for what felt like forever. She, too, probably felt helpless, but she provided a place of strength and love that comforted me more than she will ever know. She tried to convince me to go home, but I wouldn't. I had a job to do, and I wanted to pretend this wasn't happening. The next few hours at work would be the last time I could pretend this wasn't happening, so I was going to stay at work. I wanted to feel normal for as long as I would be allowed.

When I went back to my office, a student walked in to talk about some problem she had. I looked at her quizzically. It didn't quite register with me that the world was still moving. Didn't people know my life had just been shattered? I felt like everything was moving in slow motion. Thankfully, teenagers are self-absorbed so the student did not notice my bloodshot eyes. Somehow, I was able to have a coherent conversation with her. That student, whom I remember vividly, had no idea that she helped me feel normal for a minute. For a second, I was the counselor I was at 7:59 AM. I allowed myself to be absorbed in her story, and it was as therapeutic for me as it was for her.

But then it was 10:00 AM and I had to leave. I had to walk out of work and leave behind every definition I placed on myself and become a cancer patient. My life before cancer was ending. I was moving into a new chapter. One that I was not so anxious to read.

Chapter 2
And So It Begins

When I got home, my husband was waiting for me with a look on his face that I have never seen. It was a look of confusion coupled with fear and sadness. Apparently, he had taken the news of my cancer to mean that I was going to die. He was going through different scenarios of single parenthood. How was he going to tell Jacob, how was he going to pay the bills, what would his life look like without me in it? On some level, I think learning I was not going to die from this diagnosis provided a sense of relief for him that would not have existed had he not first gone through the widowed dad scenario.

The look on Joe's face softened when he realized the look on mine was covered in fear. Like most partners of those going through cancer, he felt an immediate and strong impulse to protect me. We embraced. I cried. We drove to the doctor in silence. I think we both felt that breathing air into this new world would give it life. If we just remained silent, maybe we would get to the doctor and they would tell us it was all a mistake. And maybe the pope is Protestant.

When we arrived, we were walked back to a private office and told to have a seat. We were left there for a few minutes alone. I found myself surveying the walls. I saw pictures of three beautiful children, all with very dark, beautiful hair. I found myself fixated on their hair. At some point, I realized I was running my fingers through mine, holding on to it for fear that I might not see it for much longer. When my doctor came into the office, she sat down and got right to it.

I appreciated that about her. I mean, who wants to have small talk at a time like this? She told me I had stage 2 breast cancer. It was HER2 positive. I couldn't help but think about how funny that sounded. Why not HIM2 positive? She didn't really have much else to tell me at that point. Instead, she referred me to an oncologist. She already made an appointment for 4 PM. That was a little concerning. So I guess the rule is, when it is serious, the doctors make the appointments for you. It was probably a good call though. Left to my own devices, I probably never would have called. I have this odd fear of doctors because I am afraid they will tell me something is wrong. It is counterintuitive, I know.

As we got in the car to drive off to what was about to be the beginning of an endless amount of doctor's appointments, our joint concern was how we would handle this with Jacob. Our eight-year-old got out of school at 4:00. Joe ended up calling his mom. At first, I didn't want him to tell her what was happening. I was still in denial and thought that when I got to the oncologist, he would tell me this was not that big of a deal. I quickly realized this was not reality and acquiesced. Joe's mom jumped to the rescue, as she often has in times of crisis, and offered to pick up Jacob and meet us at our house after our appointment.

As we walked into the medical building that would soon feel like a second home to me, it felt so surreal. I was 43 years old. I exercised, I ate reasonably, I had no history of cancer. Surely, they looked at someone else's files and mixed it up with mine.

My oncologist had a great bedside manner. You could tell he had some experience with the emotional aftermath of a cancer diagnosis. But he was still a doctor and started rattling on about what my type of cancer was and how they have treated it with surgery and radiation. My spirits started to lift. The weight on my shoulders became lighter. I did not hear the word *chemotherapy*, and if I didn't hear chemotherapy, that meant I was not going to lose my hair, and if I wasn't going to lose my hair then I could still be the tall, thin, pretty blonde. This was fine. I could do this type of cancer. I could do surgery and radiation. I began to feel like myself again.

But then he said because my cancer was so invasive and so aggressive, we were going to start with chemotherapy. Waterworks. I mean, uncontrollable tears. No longer at the thought of cancer, but at the thought of losing my hair. My identity was going to be taken away. Who was I if I was not pretty? How would I hide behind my mask when my mask was being ripped from me?

The next day at 9 AM, the phone calls started coming in. Doctors kept calling me to schedule appointments. I no longer had control over what time or what day my appointments were. It was as if I was a prisoner locked behind the bars of my diagnosis. I was at the mercy of the medical field. This was new territory to me on so many levels. For me, the inability to control my circumstances created a very real anxiety. I wouldn't say that I am a controlling person in the sense that I need to know what is going on around me at all times. However, there is an element of comfort in being able to decide my own schedule. This comfort was ripped from me like a Band-Aid off the skin. I suddenly felt like I was walking through a foreign country in which I did not understand the language.

I received phone call after phone call to schedule MRI's, CT scans, echocardiograms, surgeries. I would frantically write down appointment times, parking instructions, and items I needed to make sure I had with me. It was overwhelming. My head was spinning just as fast as my reality. I wanted to go back. I didn't want to know about this life with cancer. I didn't want to hear about how things happen for reasons, or how this would change me for the better. I didn't want to be positive. I felt mad, sad, and vulnerable. I was in mourning over the plans I had made before cancer, I was grieving over the eventual loss of my hair, my privacy, and what felt like parts of my dignity. I did not feel strong.

I did not feel like one of those people who rise above situations to come out the other side a better person. I felt weak. I felt like cancer was going to take from me my value as a person. In a minute, I was going to be without hair, and I was terrified that I would finally be found out. People would know for certain that I had no idea what I was doing. What did I bring to the table if I was not the pretty one?

Chapter 3

Fearless is a Stupid Word

As people found out about my diagnosis, they told me I was handling it well, but I was not. I cried all the time. I cried in the middle of the night, on my way to work, and from work. During the day, I would put on my game face, as educators often do. But when no one was looking, I would cry. I was afraid and I couldn't stop crying.

Everywhere I looked, I saw the word fearless when describing cancer. "Be Fearless." I saw it on keychains, T-shirts, mugs, tattoos. Fearless is a stupid word. If you are going through anything tragic and you don't have fear, you might be a robot. I was afraid. I was terrified. I was sometimes paralyzed to even think or move. When I thought of what lay ahead of me, I pictured a mountain, and I didn't know if I had the right climbing shoes. I would move forward, one foot at a time, and hoped I didn't slip. Some people might call that fearless. I called it life. I was just a woman with cancer, who didn't want to have cancer, doing the things that needed to be done so that I wouldn't have cancer. That's it.

If you ever question whether you are on display, try having cancer. It suddenly becomes the only thing that anyone wants to talk about. I had become one giant cancer cell, apparently with a note on my head reading, "Ask me how I'm doing." I realize this question comes from a place of good, but the news of my cancer was way too raw for me to process how I was doing, much less be able to talk about it with anyone. So please, if you know someone with cancer, stop asking them how they are doing. They have cancer. They are not doing well.

One of the hardest parts for me about getting my cancer diagnosis was having to tell my son. He was eight years old at the time. Full of life and optimism, not understanding that sometimes life throws curveballs at you when you are not wearing a mitt. How would I let him know this was happening to me without making him worry? The answer was that I wasn't. A child is going to worry when you tell them you have this thing that will seem to take the life out of you, with the hope that it will eventually put the life back into you.

A friend of mine suggested that I not use the word "sick." Sickness implies it is contagious (at least it does to an eight-year-old mind). We did not want my son to think he could catch this, so we resorted to simply calling it what it is: cancer. We have never been into mincing words, so why start now? He loves Star Wars, so we told him the medicine I had to take to make me better was also going to make me lose my hair, but not to worry because the cancer is like Darth Vader and the medicine is like Han Solo. So when he sees my hair fall out, he can feel happy because that means that the good guys are winning. He asked a few questions and cried a little as he struggled to wrap his little head around what he was just told, but he seemed to handle it well. In the months that followed, he would periodically ask questions about what was going on. We decided to answer them as they came up and do what we could to make the year that lay ahead of us as normal as possible for him.

Chapter 4
I'm not Crying, You're Crying

On May 15, my cancer treatment officially started with an MRI. They scheduled it for 7 PM at night—what an odd time to be going to the doctor. Because it was scheduled for the evening, I decided to go to work. At that point, the only people at work who knew about my diagnosis were my fellow school counselors, the secretaries, and the administrative team. I also shared it with a few of my teacher friends.

I am an introvert by nature. If you know Meyers Briggs Personality Indicator, I am an INFJ. I like to keep my story close to my chest, sharing it with only trusted confidantes. I do not like attention being drawn to me, and I don't like small talk. The burden of having cancer came with a bigger diagnosis. I would have to be out in the open. I mean, you can't lose your hair and not have people notice. This horrible thing would force me to be polite when I wanted to scream. I would have to endure repetitive stories about someone else's experience with breast cancer. Ultimately though, I felt I would have to be the one who made other people feel comfortable being around me. People would look at me with pity and become mute. It would be my role to assure them that I was fine. Cancer was not only going to take away my identity; it would take away all my energy. I was sure I would leave work every day with an introvert hangover.

I hate walking into a situation right after something significant happens. I don't even like it after I just get a haircut because I don't like people commenting. Cancer is a bit bigger than cutting three inches off my hair. As it turns out, my coworkers were just as apprehensive to ask me about it as I was to tell them about it. No one said anything, which was even more awkward. Finally, when we were all together at lunch, I broke the ice. I realized if I didn't bring it up, they wouldn't either, and then there would be a 5,000-ton elephant in the room. So I just randomly started talking about my diagnosis, which opened up the dialogue and allowed people to ask questions. Phew! Glad that part was over. I somehow made it through the day. Not without bouts of tears, but I made it. Sometimes we can count a victory just because we showed up. That was one of those days.

When I got home, my in-laws were already there with dinner prepared. My mother-in-law, Alice is always good for a meal and a listening ear. Honestly, I do not know how I would have gotten through those first few days without her and Derryl (Joe's stepdad). They ate dinner with us and stayed with Jacob while Joe and I went to the hospital for my MRI.

I cried the whole car ride there. When I got there, they made me change into a hospital gown and wait. I cried again. They finally called me into the room, which consisted of a giant tube and a gurney-like thing that I was to lay on while they slowly slid me into the tube to take a closer look. They asked me what type of music I liked to listen to because they were going to stream it into this dark tunnel of despair in hopes that it would somehow make me feel calm. I told them I liked easy listening, but they might as well have had heavy metal on. It would have mirrored how I felt better than Lionel Richie singing "Easy Like Sunday Morning."

The tube of doom was scary. I cried through the whole thing. Not because it hurt or because I'm claustrophobic, but because that MRI marked the beginning of all the treatments. It meant I had cancer, and I could no longer pretend that I didn't. The medical professional who did my MRI noticed the tears streaming down my face as she slid me out of the tube. Instead of ignoring it, she stopped and hugged me. I know this sounds peculiar, but it was exactly what I needed. I was scared, and I needed someone to recognize my fear. She didn't say much to me, but her embrace spoke louder than any words could have. I'm not a hugger by nature, but that embrace was one of the most meaningful that I will remember in my life. I don't know what the woman's name was, and I barely remember what she looked like, but I will always remember how she made me feel that day my world caved in around me.

I got dressed and came out to greet my husband, who was scrolling through his phone to distract him from what was happening to me on the other side of the door. The poor man had seen me cry more times in the last two weeks than he had for the entirety of our 17 years of marriage. He asked if I was okay; I wasn't. We walked in silence to the car and drove home. Tomorrow was another day. I would try again to pretend this wasn't happening.

Lezah was the only person at work that I let my guard down in front of. She is my colleague, but more than that, she is one of my best friends. When I got to work on May 16th, a lot of people asked me how it went. I said it went fine. Lezah came into my office, shut the door, and simply asked, "How are you really doing?" I told her that I was not handling this well and I know how vain it sounded to be so upset about losing my hair, but I was just so terrified of being ugly. She let me have that feeling because she knew that it was not vanity, but a lack of security in who I was without my hair that drove my fear. She sat and listened to me cry. Little did I know she was going through a lot in her own life at the time of my diagnosis. She never let on though. She is the true picture of selflessness. She knew there would be a time when I would be the one to be there for her, but right then it was her turn. Everyone needs a friend like Lezah.

It didn't take long before the small weight, that had been lifted after talking to Lezah, found itself back on my shoulders. Not because of the questions that people asked, but because of their anecdotes. People don't like feeling helpless. This becomes even more clear when they are trying to support you through an illness or diagnosis. If I had a dime for every time someone offered a story about someone they know who has or had breast cancer, and how they are doing fine now, I would be rich. I'm unclear what your mother's, sister's, or friend's cancer has to do with me. Also, telling me all these stories normalizes breast cancer. It makes it feel common, and therefore not something I should make such a big deal out of. But it is a big deal. This is MY cancer. This is the first time it is happening to me, and I want to be able to have my own story, unclouded by those who went before me.

This cancer. My cancer. It is so much more than everyone else's cancer. It is more than thinking I would come out the other side with a clean bill of health. My cancer doesn't symbolize mortality. For whatever reason, I always knew I would be okay. No, *my* cancer symbolized the loss of everything I knew myself to be. My cancer symbolized years of struggling to get pregnant and years of failed fertility attempts. Because my cancer was likely caused by all the infertility treatments, it brings to the surface eight years of heartache, only to be met with something that wanted to destroy me.

We all have our own stories that precede our cancer diagnosis. Everybody's cancer is their own cancer. Everybody's cancer brings to the surface all the vulnerable emotions that lay dormant while they were busy living their lives. Please allow us to have our own experience.

Chapter 5

Frozen Heads and Stupid Questions

It's funny how when you get diagnosed with cancer, doctors don't wait for reality to catch up with you. Trying to gather a semblance of understanding is futile when you don't have a moment to sit and reflect. The rare times I did have to myself, all I could do was cry.

The thing about grief is that it is not reserved for the dead. The grieving cycle happens whether death is metaphorical or real. In my case, it felt like both. While thankfully, I was not physically dying, the person whom I always saw myself to be was soon to be gone. Because of that, I was grieving who she was. The fear of the unknown was paralyzing. I spent my spare moments crying in private. I wasn't ready to move forward. I didn't have the luxury of standing still. Where do I go from here? I go to the oncologist, that's where.

My oncologist knew how difficult losing my hair would be for me. Probably because every time he mentioned it, my tears would well up. He mentioned that there was a way that I could keep my hair. WHAT? Why was I just learning about this? For a minute, I felt just as I did before I was told I had to do chemotherapy: relieved.

I have come to terms with the fact that doctors are like salesmen. First, they tell you all the good news for the buy-in, and then they tell you that basically none of that good news will work unless, unless, unless.

I was told that I could use a cold cap to keep my hair. This means that I would have to wear a freezing cold ice pack for eight hours each chemo session. EIGHT HOURS! It would hurt. Then, I couldn't dye my hair or style it as usual during chemo and for six months afterward. So I would have dull hair with gray highlights that would look bad. And on top of that, it would cost about $300 a month for the rental fee for the cap itself and $150 a month for the person who helps adjust it. I had to do six rounds of chemo, which would equate to five months. This is a lot of money to end up looking ugly anyway. I was now in a no-win situation.

So I decided to go with the loss that wouldn't dig into my bank account. So I elected to lose my hair. I could get a pretty wig that wouldn't be gray or dull blonde, or I could get a pretty scarf that I could change up daily. This also meant my treatments would be two hours instead of eight. Well, they TOLD me they would be two hours. That was another salesman tactic.

My first chemo was scheduled for May 31st. My last would be in mid-September. The doctor told me the effects wouldn't be too bad, and that I could resume normal activity. But I would be bald. Nothing would be normal anymore. I'm wondering how the doctor knows how my results would be when he has never had chemotherapy. Everybody's an expert, I guess.

So at that point, I had been to a lot of doctors. I had waited in a lot of waiting rooms. I had read a lot of pamphlets, filled out a lot of forms, and spoken with a lot of other patients. I had noticed some things. I preface this by saying that I am a counselor, so perhaps these observations are only apparent to me because I am always looking out for words and phrases that might be offensive to other people. Turns out, medical offices have a lot of these. Here are some of the questions that have been asked of me via the patient input forms I have had to fill out:

1. *Do you have children?*
2. *How many times have you been pregnant?*
3. *How many live births?*

So let's dissect this one. I adopted, so the fact that I have children is irrelevant to your question. You can omit that. What you really want to know is if I can get pregnant and if I can deliver a healthy child. I refuse to say I don't have children, so what happens is a quizzical look from the nurse when she reads over my responses. This, I rather enjoy. I am a mother and I refuse to say I do not have children to satisfy your questionnaire.

Here is another one:

Do you have a history of cancer?

Hmm. I have cancer NOW, but I have not had it before. How do I answer? Simple solution here, and it involves a two-part question:

Do you currently have cancer?
Have you ever had cancer in the past?

One more:

Are you male or female?

This is shortsighted and offensive to those who identify as neither. It needs to have "transgender," "other," "prefer not to respond." I decided when this was all over, I would tell the doctors they needed to change the questions they ask patients. But at that time, I would make note of all the shortsightedness there is in a field that is supposed to be all-knowing. Somehow, this gave me back a little bit of control, and at that point, feeling a little bit in control of my life felt nice.

Chapter 6

Don't Forget About the Caretaker

As the weeks went on, I realized that cancer brings out a lot of awkwardness in everyone I encountered. People don't know how to deal with problems that they do not have power to solve. I have come into this with a deeper understanding of people than I did when I went through infertility so many years ago. Back then, I expected everyone to support me in the way I needed. Consequently, I ended up losing friends who could not give me what I needed.

This time around, I was wiser. I no longer expected all my friends to fit in the same box. They are all valuable and I love them all. Some are great at emotional support, and some have no emotional support to give, but they will cook, watch my kid, or do other tasks that are equally helpful. All of these people are equally important to me. I think when going through any kind of life-changing event, it is imperative to know your audience. This will avoid disappointment. I don't have to expect a cow to produce an egg.

I worried about Joe a lot. He was trying to be strong for me, but he was stressed out. Forgetting things that are routine. He started breaking out in hives. Eating more, moving less. People forget that cancer happens to more than one person; it happens to a whole family. But for the spouse, it becomes brutal. Joe, like any spouse I would imagine, had feelings of helplessness and fear that are not recognized. They often have to pick up the slack, and this makes them tired too. In some ways, the caregiver has it harder than the patient. Sure, I was facing a challenge, but Joe was too. As my spouse, he wanted to fix it. It pained him to see me going through so much pain and not be able to do anything about it.

Joe already had to watch me go through fertility treatments that required many drugs and medication that caused a plethora of unwelcome side effects. He watched me in tears as my body was treated as a science experiment, only in the end to have failing results after failing results. And now, he had to watch me go through cancer. At one point, he actually told me he felt bad because I was the one who had to keep going through these things. The guilt that the cancer patient's spouse feels must be overwhelming. Joe is an evolved man. But no matter how evolved the man is, he has the innate need to fix things. This could not be fixed. Joe's mantra has always been "It will all work out." This time, he didn't know if it would. This time, even if it did, he would have to watch me suffer as I went through it.

Chapter 7

Tears

Things started happening very quickly. I got a CT scan and echocardiogram one day and my port insertion the next. They apparently insert ports now so they don't destroy your veins when running chemo juice through your system. My port was inserted on the area between my shoulder and breast on my left side.

It seems that every time I went to a procedure, I would start crying. When I arrived at the hospital for my port insertion, they checked me in and walked me over to a private room where I lay down on a bed in a hospital gown. A few nurses stopped by to check my vitals. I tried to hold it together as best as I could, but by the time the third nurse came in to tell me about what would be happening, I could feel the tears slowly streaming down my cheek.

This woman, much like the woman who did my MRI, took notice enough to stop what she was saying so I could have my feelings. She acknowledged that this was scary and agreed with me when I told her how scared I was to lose my hair. She didn't try to talk me out of my feelings. Instead, she gently placed her hand on my shoulder and allowed me to cry real, unfiltered tears. After a while, I learned that she had breast cancer herself. I felt an immediate sisterhood with her.

With every procedure, I knew I was less likely to hide from the world. The MRI reminded me that this was happening, but the port served as a visual reminder to the world. The anesthesiologist is the last doctor I remember seeing. The next thing I remember, I was lying on the hospital bed and there was a foreign object the size of a golf ball on my left side.

I had to take the next day off of work because the residual effects from the anesthesia were horrible. Joe took the day off too so he could help with anything I needed. I slept the entire day. This marked the first day that I was unable to function at normal capacity due to this stupid thing. Not even at my first chemo and I already felt helpless.

Joe refused to talk to me about it. He seemed to think that it was not fair for him to have worries when I had cancer. I reached out to his brothers, asking them to check in on him every now and again. He might not have felt okay talking to me, but he is close to all of his brothers, and I knew they could provide some sense of relief for him.

I kept looking at the basket of chemo supplies that were given to me—things that were supposed to comfort me. I just keep looking at it. I saw body lotion, ginger ale, and Chap Stick. In a few days, I would have to open it. In a few days, all of this would become real. In a few days, I would start waking up every morning just waiting for my hair to fall out—waiting for my life to change.

I bought a wig in preparation for my impending baldness. I had not yet decided if I would wear it, but I wanted it there just in case. After all, when I did eventually lose my hair, I would need to have some headwear possibilities on hand. I also bought a bunch of chemo scarves to add to the growing collection that had been given to me by so many people after they found out about my cancer. Scarves and blankets. This seems to be the gift of choice for cancer patients.

Chapter 8
Round 1 of Chemo

After weeks of anticipation, the first day of chemotherapy was almost here. The day before was riddled with anxiety. As one would expect, I did not sleep well the night before. I didn't know what to expect. I had always heard about how sick chemotherapy made people. It might stand to reason that I would get used to the uncertainty that this diagnosis brings at some point, but that day had not yet come. I found myself still trying to grasp at any amount of certainty that I could get so that I could feel a little bit in control. But as it turned out, control seemed to be the first thing to go. Even before the hair.

At 8:00 AM on May 31st, 2017, I walked into the chemo office. I came prepared with a bag of supplies, a blanket, and my husband. As we walked in, I took a moment to survey who was there with me. Some women, some men. All of them looked older than me. Some of them had their hair, some of them didn't. After I filled out the intake form, which asked me a bunch of questions about how I was feeling and would be the form that I would fill out for each time I visited this office, I was taken back to get my weight and height, my blood drawn, and the IV put into my port. From there, I was guided toward a private office where I was to sit and wait for my oncologist to arrive. The moments before his arrival were frightening to say the least. Not knowing what to expect had me expecting the worse. Joe and I sat in silence.

When the doctor arrived, he explained how long the procedure would take and what kind of side effects I might experience. He said whatever I experience in the first round would likely be what I experience in all rounds. This proved to be false. Each round brought with it different gifts. As my body began to get worn down by all the chemotherapy drugs, it meant that my side effects became worse with each round. I do not know if this is protocol for everyone, but that is what it was like for me.

The doctor walked Joe and me back to the room where cancer was treated. It looked just as I envisioned it would: recliner chairs lined against the wall with IV poles on rollers next to them. As I looked around the room, I saw men and women of all ages hooked up to these IVs. Everyone had different amounts of bags attached to them. I was to have five bags.

They gave me Benadryl to start. It works in conjunction with another anti-nausea medicine. The upside is that it made me feel high, which is not a feeling I have had before. I suddenly got very giggly and started slurring my words. My leg felt as if it were 60 pounds. Joe found it quite funny. Thankfully, it also made me fall asleep for about an hour and a half, which is good because the whole process took over five hours. Did you hear that? FIVE HOURS. Not two hours. FIVE!

Drugs will kill you unless you have cancer, then they will heal you. In my case, I enjoyed a cocktail of a variety of very specific mixers. I would've preferred them served over ice, but my doctor insisted on giving them to me through an IV. I was given four drugs in addition to Benadryl. They come in a specific order, but I don't know what it is because I was asleep the whole time. I would've asked, but I didn't care. This is generally the same reason I don't ask lots of questions in my life.

All of the following drugs are used for the treatment of HER2-positive breast cancer, which is what I have.

Perjeta
There are potentially 28 side effects of this drug. I won't list them all, but they include hair loss, diarrhea, nausea, fatigue, rash, decreased appetite, swelling, shortness of breath, headache, dizziness, vomiting, abnormal taste, and dry skin.

Herceptin
There are potentially 24 side effects for this drug. They include all of the same as Perjeta.

Carboplatin
26 potential side effects. Many are the same as previously noted, but also include taste changes, constipation, mouth sores, and numbness or tingling.

Taxotere
There are 23 potential side effects for this drug. All of them are included in what was noted for Perjeta but also include fluid retention, nail changes, low platelet count, and allergic reactions.

After happy hour at the chemo bar, I got a prescription for steroids, which I was supposed to take for two days. Then, I got Neulasta. This is a huge square object that I got to wear on my arm for 28 hours. It shot more drugs into me that were supposed to help with nausea.

The doctor said if I had side effects, which I most likely would, I would see them in about three to seven days after treatment. My hair would start thinning in about two and a half weeks. Then it would just fall out unless I was one of the lucky ones who just get thinning hair, but that couldn't look good either.

The days that followed chemotherapy, I sat in anticipation. Waiting to get sick. Constantly checking my hair for signs of thinning. It is very unsettling to know that you are going to get sick, but you just don't know when.

The first day after chemo, I felt pretty good. I'd rate myself at about 90%. I did have a massive headache overnight, which kept me up for about two hours. But I got up at 4:45 to exercise, had a protein shake along with a steroid pill, and went about my day. Ironically, I had one of the best hair days that I had in a while that day. Life is full of cruel jokes.

The second day after chemo was a little more intense. The anticipation of being sick might have made me sick. I actually felt fine when I think about it, but I kept thinking "In three to seven days, I will have side effects." The first round of chemo seems like it might be the worst because you have no indication of when these side effects will occur. Nor do you know what they will be, how severe they will be, or how long they will last.

I was literally just waiting to be sick. Waiting for my hair to start thinning. Someone told me I looked like I might be sick, which is a little insulting because I actually thought I looked really good. It made me wonder if other people were also anticipating the onset of chemo reactions. I was already the cancer patient. People were waiting for me to look the part just as I was.

A few of my scarves came in the mail. I tried them on. Nope. Not gonna look good bald. Everyone would tell me I do because how mean would it be to say "Dude, that's gross. You should have hair." But I'm pretty sure they would be lying. What they would want to say is "For someone who doesn't have hair, you're making it look alright." Because if any woman could make bald look better than hair, wouldn't most women choose to be bald?

By the third day, I started having a slight reaction to food. It's a bummer because I really like food. It just didn't settle well. Unfortunately, the day food became the enemy was also graduation day at the high school where I worked at the time. I called the names at graduation, and although all of my administrators from work told me I didn't have to, it was really important for me to do it. I had been calling names at graduation for at least seven years. That would not be the year I stopped.

I took a shower and did my hair. It looked really good. Figures. As I drove to the graduation venue, I started crying. That was probably the last public setting that I would be able to enter without people knowing I had cancer.

As I arrived, people told me I looked nice. They wouldn't tell me that for much longer. People told me that my hair looked good. Time was running out on that too.

Soon, I wouldn't be pretty. I would be the girl with cancer. People would look at me with pity. This could've all been in my head, but it was my perception. And right then, it was also my reality. If I said this out loud to anyone, they would argue with me and tell me I was being irrational. But if you were to lose your legs, would it be irrational for you to think that you could no longer run marathons? People judge a book by its cover. My cover was my hair.

Chapter 9

Everything Tastes Gross

Okay, now I couldn't feel my tongue. I was about five days in and my tongue felt like cotton balls. My gums were sensitive and I couldn't drink coffee. Really? Cancer is taking away my hair AND my coffee. Okay, fine. But I draw the line at wine. If you take away my wine, we will have some words.

Everything was beginning to taste like metal. Everything. At one point, I was finding myself craving fried cheese. My plan was to make some and watch *The Real Housewives of New York*. Mindless TV about the problems of upper-class New Yorkers might help me put my own life into perspective. But cancer had other plans. Suddenly, fried cheese tasted like metal. This was getting really depressing. I knew chemo would take my hair, but I wasn't prepared for it to take away my food.

I started writing down my symptoms every day. I hoped doing this would help me know what to expect for the rounds of chemo to come. Or it could be because cancer had left me feeling out of control, and this was my way of giving it the middle finger and telling it that I still get to control some things. Anyway, so far I had been lucky. Besides some minor stomach inconveniences and the general numbness and metal taste, I was still doing pretty well. I still had my hair, although I noticed it had been thinning some. I still woke up at 4:45 AM to work out every morning and go to work every day.

Considering some people are debilitated, I marked this as a win. Not that I believe in comparing my experience to others who may have had a worse experience. I feel like doing that negates the personal experiences that we have. I hate that 'it could be worse' mentality. F – that. It could be better too. In any case, I recognized the symptoms could've been more severe. I also recognized that I was only on day six.

I couldn't seem to acquiesce to my treatment. I wanted so badly to be normal, whatever that meant. I just wanted to go back to being the tall, thin, pretty blonde. I was so afraid of losing all of me, that I held tightly to the pieces of me that I could still control a little. I hoped I could keep up some semblance of a routine when I was deeper into the treatment.

As the days went on, my physical appearance was starting to wane. Not only did I have a port inserted in my shoulder that bulged out for all to see (and a nice scar to go along with it), but now I had a giant rash on the left side of my arm. Cancer really would have fit better into my schedule if it happened in winter when I could wear long sleeves. Maybe next my lips would become so chapped they would bleed when I smiled. Or better yet, my bald head would be super lumpy so that I looked like a cone head. The excitement was killing me. I couldn't wait. WTF!

I called the doctor about said rash, just to make sure this was a normal reaction to chemo and to see if I could just pick up some over the counter aid on my way home. Before the cancer, I hated going to the doctor for anything. There was a strong part of me that didn't even want to mention this rather ugly rash to the doctor now. Ultimately, the rational side of me won. Or maybe it was more of my husband's rational side that kept pestering me to call. Stuck between the constant questions from my husband and going to the doctor, I chose going to the doctor. After all, maybe it was something significant.

Making appointments to see the doctor can be a lesson in patience. First, let me say that I have had many good experiences with receptionists over the years. More good than bad, actually. But for some reason, the receptionists from my oncologist's office got very irritated when they are asked a question.

I feel like if you are a receptionist at a medical facility that treats cancer patients, it might be a good idea to have a soothing voice instead of the voice of annoyance. When I called, I told the receptionist what I was experiencing and her response was, "That's it?"

So I immediately got all self-conscious and thought, "Oh, well, I guess it is silly to call about a rash."

Perhaps, dear receptionist, you should have said, "Okay, is there anything else that you are experiencing that I can let the doctor know about?" So then she just says, "Okay."

What? What do you mean, "Okay?" That's it? You're done? At that point, I realized I was the facilitator of that phone call and the one required to ask all the questions. So I asked, "Soooo…are you leaving a message? Is someone going to call me back?"

"Yep," she said.

"Okay...do you want my phone number?"

"I'm looking at your chart," she said.

Well, alrighty then. Of course you are. Thank you for being so cooperative and not at all making me feel like a total jackass for calling. I for sure will feel confident that this exchange will go to the hands of the appropriate medical professional.

But it turns out that the joke was on the nonchalant receptionist who was annoyed that I would call for a silly rash. Turns out the doctor did not think it was silly and actually wanted to see me later on the same day. Unfortunately, it was also at the same time Jacob got out of school. Cancer does not care that you have a life. Doctors don't really care either. They want to see you when they want to see you.

Turns out I had folliculitis, which is basically the poison attacking my hair follicles in my arm. Perhaps I wouldn't have to worry about waxing my upper lip anymore. I would, however, still have to shave my legs. Apparently, the hair is not affected on the legs. This seemed unfair. Also, the in-person receptionist was no kinder than the phone receptionist. She actually stopped talking to me mid-sentence so she could talk to another patient. Then, she looked at me like I was annoying HER. Sorry to annoy you with my cancer.

Chapter 10
It's Not Just Hair

Taking a shower had become a traumatic event. For the last two days, I had pulled out a lot of hair. I mean, A LOT. The strands were so loose in my head that I could barely brush it because every time I did, the brush took clumps of my hair hostage. Using a round brush to blow-dry was now out of the question for the same reason. So I was left to wearing it curly because it only required a diffuser and no brush. But my days were numbered with that too. Soon I would wake up to find my hair looking back at me on my pillow, and I would have to make a decision of not if, but when to shave it. But it's just hair, right? Yah, kind of in the same way that to men, a penis is just an appendage.

One way to get a cancer patient to want to punch you in the face—and there are many—is to tell them that it is just hair. Women spend thousands of dollars yearly on what is "just hair." Hair is an industry. Hair is an identity. Let me tell you a little bit about my hair.

When I was little I had long, golden blonde hair. I used to make my mom put curlers in it every night so I could wake up to beautiful waves. At one point, my mom said that she had to cut my hair because people kept telling her how cute I was with my long, blonde hair, and she didn't want my sister to feel bad (my sister was cute, but she was a tomboy, and I was every stereotype of what a girl is). My mom never gave me the message that my hair made me cute, but society did, and the message never stopped as I grew older. People have always complimented me on my hair. I had nice hair.

Aside from my hair, I have always put way too much importance on the way I look. I got the message very early on that I was cute as a child, and as I became older, I was pretty. That is the only descriptor that people would use to tell me who I was (to be fair, I am sure that people used other descriptors, but this is the one that I held on to). What happens when you get messaging like that is you develop a skewed sense of who you are.

As a result, I developed an eating disorder in my junior year of high school. I felt like all I was is pretty, so if I lost that I was nothing. My appearance helped me mask my fear of getting found out. In a minute here, I would have no hair, and I was terrified that I would finally be found out. What do I bring to the table if I am not the pretty one? This in no way, shape, or form passes the out loud test. I am fully aware of this. Logically, I knew that I had other things to bring to the table. Emotionally, it was terrifying to know that soon, I would not be described as the pretty one.

So don't tell me that it is just hair. It is not just hair. It is MY hair. It defines who I am. It is my finest accessory. Without it, I lose part of my identity. Don't tell me I will look good without hair because you don't know that. Don't minimize my emotional reaction to me losing my hair by telling me how it might grow back thicker and curlier. Don't tell me that at least it won't take me as long to get ready anymore, or to think of all the money I will save. Don't tell me at least I feel good physically, or that it is no big deal. Don't tell me that it could be worse because that is a cop-out answer. Every single situation has a 'could be worse' component to it. 'Could be worse' scenarios take away the validity of the emotion. They make the recipient feel guilty for having their feelings, and they make you look like an asshole. So don't say it. Ever. In any situation.

And for the love of God, don't tell me a story about someone else's experience with hair loss. What the hell is it with a tragic event that makes people want to tell you stories about what happened with someone else? When I was going through infertility, I had countless stories about how people adopted and then got pregnant. Umm…that's an awesome story. You may also want to include the fact that there are countless more who adopted and DID NOT get pregnant. People want to bridge a gap, I get that. But pouring me a tall glass of wine and listening to my story without your anecdotes is a more effective way to do that.

People would ask me how I was doing and I always said I was doing well because physically I was. What I didn't tell them was that emotionally I was a wreck. I didn't want to have this thing that threatened to strip me of my dignity and leave in its place a void I wasn't sure I knew how to fill. I didn't want to do chemo, surgery, and radiation. I didn't want to forever be worried if the cancer would return. But mostly, I didn't want to lose my hair.

When chemo became a part of my treatment plan and it was determined that I would lose my hair, many people suggested I cut it short so that it would not be so traumatic. Even books and articles I read from those who went before me suggested doing this. I, however, was resistant. To me, having ugly hair before I have ugly hair did not make sense. Equally, cutting it short and falling in love with it weeks before it would fall out seemed worse. Ultimately, I decided to keep all of my hair until it became evident I could no longer do so and still manage an element of cuteness.

Taking a shower had become interesting. What I left behind looked like a grizzly bear decided to wash itself off. Every morning, I was continually impressed that so much hair could fall out without me feeling anything. I mean, wasn't it coming out of my scalp? Shouldn't that hurt? I read somewhere that for some, the hair falling out feels like you have the flu in your head. I guess that makes sense, kinda. Your scalp *is* vomiting out hair, and then when you feel like it is done falling out for the day, you go to run your fingers through it and take out another gigantic chunk. It's really a fun game. Hair spray became a necessity instead of a luxury. Now I used it not to hold the style, but to keep it from falling out.

When your hair is falling out, you really need to be cognizant of the color of clothes you wear. I chose black a lot. Probably as a subconscious way to tell the world about my grief. Nonetheless, wearing black is a bad choice. It only takes a matter of minutes for your once clean, black shirt to look like a young cat just died on your shoulders.

But even with my hair shedding all over me, my decision to not cut it and just let it fall out until I couldn't take it anymore proved to be a wise one. I am glad I did not listen to all the people who suggested I might regret doing so. What I found is that my hair was becoming so gross that I was losing my love for it. And when you are about to lose your hair completely, you might find it easier when it looks bad. It's kind of like when you are about to break up with someone. It is so much easier when you hate them than it is when you love them. Every person has to decide what they're going to do to keep their sanity intact for as long as possible. What my friend does might be something different than what I do. Same goes for chemo hair. Only you can decide what is right for you. This was right for me.

There may be another reason people say you should cut your hair short before it falls out. Turns out it becomes a matted mess. I found this out the hard way one day. I slathered my hair with a conditioner three times in the shower, and I was still unable to pull a knot apart. This could have been because at that point, the matted mess was just sitting on other strands of hair and not at all connected to my scalp. So for that reason alone, I would recommend cutting your hair short if you know it's going to fall out.

Also for that reason, I decided that day was the day I lost my hair.

So while my hair was still wet, I handed Joe a pair of kitchen scissors and asked him to cut it off. I turned around so as not to look at myself in the mirror while Joe methodically chopped it off, giving no regard to aesthetics. I couldn't help but to think that this was the first step to tell the world that I have cancer. This was when it becomes public to strangers. This was when I could no longer pretend that my hair wasn't going to fall out.

As I heard each cut of the scissors I said goodbye to my old self because the truth is, even when the hair grows back, I would not be the same person as I was before it was gone. The hair that comes back will tell a deeper, more meaningful story than the hair that left. The hair that grows back will be more beautiful because it fought to get there. It will be stronger than what it left behind. Just like my hair before cancer, my hair after cancer would help define me. But in a much different way. At least this was my hope.

When Joe cut off every piece of hair that scissors would allow, he handed the razor to Jacob to make the finishing touches. My little boy grabbed the razor with a look of equal parts fear and excitement. And as the last piece was shaved off, he stood back to admire his work.

When it was over, I looked at myself in the mirror and cried. What used to be beautiful was now an ugly, nonsymmetrical mess. This felt appropriate because I too now felt like an ugly, nonsymmetrical mess. I couldn't shave it completely just yet. I still tried to hold on to what I was supposed to so easily be able to let go of.

I went to my pile of chemo hats and pretty scarves gifted to me over the last few weeks. The time had come where I had to wear them instead of just imagining what they might look like. I chose a plain gray chemo hat for my first run at this. I noticed the feeling of cotton so prominent on my scalp. It was soft, comfortable. I realized at that moment that material was suddenly going to become very important. After I put the cap on, I looked in the mirror and noticed that having no hair makes you take notice of other things. Some of these things are:

1. There's your face. Your whole face.
2. You gotta wear big earrings.
3. Bold lipstick helps.
4. Mascara has never been so important.
5. Use an eyebrow pencil to darken what has either disappeared or thinned.

If you were to ask me how I was feeling on this day, I am not sure I could have given you a really good answer. I would forget I had a scarf on, catch a glimpse of myself in the mirror, and was like, "Holy hell, I have a fivehead!" But then again, it was kind of good to just get it over with so I could get used to it and move on. The anticipation is always scarier than the event. My only regret is that it had to happen before I was done working for the summer. I wanted to have the luxury of getting used to this on my own time. But cancer strips you of the luxury of choice.

Chapter 11
I'm Bald

So now I had no hair. It was Sunday. I was to return to work for one final week before beginning summer vacation. I'd be lying if I didn't say I was a little annoyed that my hair couldn't hold out for just one more week. One more week and no one would have to see me in this state of raw vulnerability. I hadn't had time to process what was happening to me yet, and in less than 24 hours I would have to walk into the office with my head held high and pretend I was okay. I was not okay. I have never felt so exposed.

It was as if everything I feared about being found out was about to really be found out. I didn't have my beauty anymore, and therefore I had nothing. I did have the insight to send a group text out to the entire office warning them that I would not look the same on Monday as I did on Friday. I felt like giving them a heads up allowed me to have some level of control. Plus, this allowed them time to fix their faces because the last thing I wanted was to witness people's faces contorting as they tried to look natural.

Chapter 12

The Beauty of Pink

Monday morning came. In years past, I would feel excitement in knowing that I only had five more days before I had the entire summer ahead of me. I always loved the summer. It is a relaxing, peaceful time. Free of worries, filled with fun. I looked ahead at the summer of 2017 with much trepidation, worry, and fear. I was a baby on the cancer journey. I didn't know what to expect. I didn't know how much my life would be turned upside down.

As I got in the car and drove the 30 minutes to work, my thoughts were all over the place. How would people receive me? How would I be able to get through the day without crying? Would everyone think I was ugly? Would I have to explain my situation to parents that might come in looking at me strangely? I wanted to turn around and go back. I wanted to go back home. I wanted to go back to May 5th before I had cancer. I could not believe that this was my life now. I hated it, and I couldn't hide from it. All of my life, I spent hiding from things that scared me. But now I had no choice but to walk alongside my fear and hope that didn't destroy me.

When I pulled into the parking lot of the high school, my stomach was in knots. This was not going to be easy. I took a deep breath and gave myself a little pep talk. Then I got out of the car with my cute cancer hat on and walked in.

I was greeted by one of the assistant principals. I noticed he was wearing pink, which was odd because he didn't usually wear pink. He saw me and excitedly said, "Hey, MF!" (which are my initials. Isn't that fantastic?). We gave our usual fist bump, and I moved down the hallway to my office, where I noticed two more people wearing pink. My first response was that this was an odd coincidence.

How strange that three people would choose pink to wear on the same day. But still not getting it, I rounded the corner to the counseling side of the office where everyone was wearing different shades of Pink. I suddenly realized what was happening. Everyone in the office coordinated with each other to show their support by wearing Pink. This was one of the most beautiful gestures that had been done for me. I cried. Not because of the cancer, but because of the love that I felt. These people were not just my coworkers. They were my friends.

Chapter 13
Round 2 of Chemo

My second round of chemo was during my last week of work for the summer. While my first round was not awesome, my reactions were manageable. The doctor told me that whatever I experienced in the first round of chemo would likely be what I experienced for the next five (I had six in total).

The morning of chemo, round two, I got up at 4:45 AM and ran three miles. All those endorphins helped to relieve my anxiety. My appointment was at 10:30. We got to the doctor, and just like my first visit, and what would be at every visit, I was given a checklist of symptoms to check off what was affecting me. So far, nothing too bad. Some diarrhea and fatigue. I felt a little lethargic, but nothing too bad. I filled in the form and gave it back to the receptionist. Then I sat in the waiting room with my husband. We sat, and sat, and sat.

At about 11:15, they called me in the back and hooked me up to the IV. Then I had to go see the doctor so he could make sure all of my blood counts were okay, and that I was cleared to go on with the five hours of a slow poison drip that would follow.

It was 12:00 before I finally sat down in the chemo chair. They started dripping me with anti-nausea meds. Then they moved on to Benadryl (my personal fave) before they infused me with my unique brand of toxic cocktail. It is ironic to me that poison can make you healthy. Some seasoned professional chemo goers joked with the nurses. They had agreed to let him start his own IV that time because he was sure he could do it better than they could. I liked listening to people in this sterile, cancer-filled room laugh and joke. It provided a little hope and a little normalcy. Life inside this club is unique for sure, but watching those who have been doing this for a while laugh and smile brought me a joy that would otherwise go unrecognized.

Almost everyone in the room was bald. That gave me peace and made me feel like I was with my people. Here, I have no shame, embarrassment, or need to give an explanation. Here, everyone was going through a similar experience. In this place was where our stories met, and we had a reprieve from explanation, from questions. Here we could just be. We were all suffering from cancer. I didn't know anyone there, but I was bonded with everyone.

Everyone seemed to know the nurses. I heard them asking how their kid was doing in baseball, how that new recipe that they were going to try worked out. This brought me hope and a little trepidation. Hope to know that maybe one day this would be me. Maybe I would be known by my name, my hobbies, or my family. It also brought a little trepidation because I know the reason they knew each other so well was that they had been coming there for so long, and I realized that this would also be me.

It didn't take long after they added Benadryl for me to lose feeling in my fingers. My legs got heavy, and my mouth felt like a ton of bricks. It actually took effort to open my mouth, and when I did get so lucky as to be able to form words, they were slurred. In a minute, I would be high and giggly and my legs would feel so heavy that I couldn't use them. I would enjoy all of these sensations because they gave me a minute to enjoy this nasty, invasive procedure and because I knew when it wore off I would take a really deep nap, making the time go faster.

I slept the entire time. The nurse had to wake me up to tell me it was over. Apparently, Joe went grocery shopping and ran some errands while I slept. I would like to say that I woke up feeling refreshed, but quite the opposite happened. I woke up feeling extremely groggy and tired. And I had a killer headache. If this was like last time, I was also going to have a headache that would keep me up all night. It's like a hangover without any of the fun stories. I was super bloated, which is a horrible feeling because no matter how little I ate, I constantly felt fat. For someone who once suffered from an eating disorder, this is a devastating feeling and could have potentially been a trigger if I was not careful.

The last round of chemo, I wrote down every one of my daily symptoms in a journal, so I found a little control in knowing I could refer back to it to see what to expect on which day. The RN told me aside from fatigue, which will progressively get worse, the symptoms will be the same. I hoped that was true. But the headache I was experiencing made me want to decapitate myself. But then I would be dead, and that would be worse than having chemo. Round two of chemo was done. Four more to go.

Remember how the doctor and the RN told me that my side effects would be the same from treatment to treatment? Yah. If the same actually means the opposite of the same.

The day after chemo I felt great, as I did the last round. But three days post-chemo, I was up for half the night with every sort of stomach issue you can imagine. I mean, vomiting, diarrhea. Think of food poisoning. There, now you know what it felt like.

Consequently, all of my energy was zapped, and I spent the entire next day sleeping. Seeing as I changed my chemo appointments from Wednesdays to Thursdays under the impression that I would feel less than perfect on days five and six, and would have the weekends to feel good, this was a very unwelcome surprise. Now I didn't know how to predict my reactions from each treatment. I could only hope that no matter how I reacted, I would be better by day eight and be gradually on the upswing until my next round of chemo. Never in my wildest imagination did I think I would be using mathematical equations to determine whether or not I would be well enough to attend a party, go on a bike ride, or just hang at the beach.

I forced myself out of bed at 8:15 on the morning of day five post-chemo. I went to bed at 8 PM, so I figured 12 hours was enough. Recognizing I was weak because I hadn't eaten, I made myself a protein-packed smoothie and drank a bunch of water. I was feeling better, although I was still somewhat in a fog of fatigue. Being tired is like an invisible illness because unlike when you are visibly ill, when you are tired you look normal. This has the potential to make you look like a slacker. But being overly tired can be just as debilitating as puking all night.

As the days went on, I was rudely made aware that not all chemos are created the same. While I was able to manage my symptoms after the first round, now it was on. I was fortunate enough to only puke once, but the diarrhea? That is no joke. Before I proceed, it is important that you understand that I am not one to even go to the bathroom with other people, much less defecate in a public place. Chemo takes your modesty pretty quickly though. When you have to go, you HAVE TO GO. I mean, find a bathroom STAT. And it is not like you take care of business and you are done. Oh no. The party keeps coming back. I was essentially pooping all day. At one point, my friend came over for a quick visit. I was in mid-conversation and had to excuse myself to use the bathroom. I know this is disgusting to read. Try living it. This is cancer.

I was being injected with four different drugs. I had seven pages of explanation about each individual drug should I ever want to know more. But I didn't want to know more. Maybe because it would scare me to know more, maybe because it wouldn't change anything anyway, or maybe I was just lazy and didn't find this interesting reading. Either way, maybe one day I will pick up the literature and read it. Maybe one day I will run a marathon too.

Anyway, the first round of chemo gave me a false sense of superpower. This gave way to the realization that I was not the superwoman I hoped I was. Along with the continual and unpredictable need to use the bathroom, I also had constant low-grade nausea and headache, coupled with a fatigue that would be debilitating if I wasn't on summer vacation and able to sleep for 12 hours a night. So along with the physical annoyances of this stupid cancer, I also got to feel like a bad mom because I just did not have the energy to keep up with Jacob. Logically, I knew that this was temporary, and within a week I would hopefully feel more like myself again. But the thought of not being able to engage with my energetic eight-year-old for an entire week spiraled me into a world of guilt. I wondered if Jacob would judge me by the weeks I was not able to engage rather than the weeks that I was. Mom guilt is no joke in a perfect situation. Add cancer and chemo to the mix, and it is an explosion of nuclear proportions.

I was hoping that as the day went on, I would start to feel better. My intent was to will myself into a healthy state. Jacob had a birthday party to go to, and I had stuff to do. This was a nice summer. The sun was out, it was hot. The beach was calling. I did not want to be sitting on my ass watching everyone else have fun around me.

Chapter 14

The Humbling Experience of Generosity

This cancer was beginning to piss me off on so many different levels. The biggest one now is that it was getting hot, and these damn scarves just make it hotter. I didn't want to walk around bald because that is not a pretty look either. I'm no Sinead O'Connor. I had to think about what I wanted to do when at the beach or a pool when I wanted to go in the water. I had a swim cap, so I guessed I could just wear that. I was annoyed that I had to think about that at all.

Also, why did I still have stubble on my head? That shit itched, and at that point, I would have rather been totally bald. At least then I could put lotion on my head so I was not constantly scratching it all day. And what kind of moron decided that I should keep the hair on my legs? One saving grace was that I had not lost my eyebrows or lashes. Small wins.

I live in a neighborhood that is straight out of *Leave it to Beaver*. It is Mayberry but on steroids. The community was designed as a co-op back in the depression when people were losing their jobs. Everyone who lives here has an acre of land that we are not allowed to sell or build another property on. The original purpose was for residents to grow their own crops and share with each other. People would carpool into work and help build each other's houses. The spirit of the neighborhood has not changed in decades. We are still a community that thrives because of our members. This neighborhood is euphoric on many levels, including the way my neighbors rallied around me when they heard of my diagnosis.

One of my neighbors organized a food train for me. The outpouring of meals that came in was humbling, to say the least. I am still craving Michelle Patterson's mac and cheese. That shit was GOOD. The problem is that I had no appetite. But even if I did, everything tasted like metal. This was a beautiful side effect that wouldn't go away for the entirety of my chemo treatment. My neighbors, along with countless friends and family who brought me food, had no way of knowing that I would be unable to eat it. But as stated previously, I forced myself to eat an entire plate of Michelle's mac and cheese. Even through my metal mouth, I could tell what it was supposed to taste like. Michelle, if you are reading this, I wouldn't mind a redo.

When things didn't taste like metal, they tasted like hot sauce. Oh, and when I swallowed, it felt like shards of glass. Sparkling beverages were the enemy. You can imagine what this does to my general disposition.

So let's get back to these scarves. They made me look like I had cancer. No matter how pretty they were, what color they were, or how expensive they were, they were for cancer patients and made my head look flat, which made my face look weird. It became daunting to think ahead and realize that this was my life for at least one full year.

Every now and again, I allowed myself to think about what lay ahead, and I wanted to scream. What if chemo was the easiest part? When it was time for radiation, I would be required to go every day for five days a week for who knows how long.

At that point, I recognized I had entered the anger phase of my grief cycle. I had a heightened awareness of how sucky this was. I was going to get to acceptance because I always did. I would take whatever lesson I was supposed to learn from that because I always do. But not right then. Right then I was just mad, and I didn't want anyone to talk me out of being mad. I wanted to punch something. I wanted to throw things, and I wanted to scream. Maybe all at the same time. I didn't want people to tell me I was handling this well. I didn't want people to tell me I looked beautiful. I didn't want people to give me words of encouragement. I just wanted to be mad. This is the face of cancer. It is ugly and angry sometimes. It is not always strong and beautiful like the commercials would have you think.

Next week, I probably wouldn't be mad anymore because the poison would be leaving my body, and I would start to feel better. I would have an appetite again and get to enjoy the delicious meals that people so generously made for me. But I am a big fan of being in your moment because if you don't sit in your moment when it happens, it will never pass. Right then, my moment was anger, and I was going to cuddle up to it like a warm blanket.

Chapter 15

Are You Staring at Me or am I Staring at You?

It started to feel like random people kept looking at me with pity or shock. My friends and family knew to give the appearance of being unfazed when they saw me. The general population was not given the memo.

I would go into random stores and pass people. I would forget I looked any different. Then I would see an adult breaking their stare when I caught them gazing at my scarf. I thought breast cancer was supposed to be so common. This is what everyone told me in a very strange attempt to try to make me feel better. If it is so common, then shouldn't I have been seeing one in four women with headscarves on? If it is so common, why were people looking at me so quizzically? Shouldn't this be commonplace? Or perhaps this is the story people need to tell so they don't sit there silently when they hear you have breast cancer.

A note of suggestion: sit there quietly while someone tells you they have breast cancer. We don't expect answers. We don't want our experience to be normalized. We recognize that you don't know what to say. We know that this is awkward for both you and us. Just say you're sorry and this sucks because those two things are genuine.

Another thing I noticed was people were extra gracious in my presence. A scarf is a superpower in itself. It transforms you into a person who is immune to the common rules of life. I could walk down the grocery store aisle, cut someone off, and *they* would apologize to *me*. Of course, these things did not happen everywhere. I could still go many places unnoticed (an introvert's dream). But it happened often enough for me to recognize.

I'm not saying that people should not have taken a second glance when they saw me. I looked different; I get that. I mean, I take a second glance when I notice someone who looks out of place. It's just that I have never been the person who looks out of place. I have done my best to blend into the walls of society so that people won't notice me. So this was all very bizarre for me. I don't like attention, especially not because of this.

Cancer is intrusive and humbling. It makes you vulnerable in a way that many don't experience. It is like a tornado. In one swoop, it snatches up your identity, your dignity, your plans, and some of your hope and peace. At some point, the tornado will pass, and you are left to rebuild a foundation that has been shaken. But by then, you will look normal again, and people will think that you are okay. But sometimes it is when things are calm again that you are really able to sit and process. Like a tornado, cancer leaves behind a new landscape. I just hoped that when my new house was built, the windows would be facing the sun.

Chapter 16
I Am My Own Flotation Device

After a while, my anger phase passed, at least for the time being. It would probably resurface again around the same time in two weeks after my next chemo. But at that time, I felt good. I felt *really* good. I guessed I could predict for the first week after chemo, I would be sluggish at best. But then around day eight, I started to feel like a human again. Except for the bloating.

I was so bloated that I had become my own floatation device. Despite not having a huge appetite, I still managed to look three months pregnant. My fingers were so swollen that I could no longer wear my wedding bands. Even my toes were bloated. If my face swelled up anymore, I might start looking like the Michelin Man. This might be comical if I didn't already struggle with body dysmorphia. It was slightly irritating that I couldn't seem to control my body. I've been trying to control my thoughts, but when so much of my thoughts are aligned with the way my body looks, it becomes a challenge.

I have heard of people gaining up to 30 pounds while on chemo. This was scary to me. Maybe even scarier than losing my hair. It definitely presented an additional mental challenge. I had to make a concerted effort not to tailspin back into the days of a restricted diet. I am self-aware enough to know who I am and what my triggers are. This helps me identify them and face them head-on. But it is not easy when I look at myself in the mirror and see a physical me I don't like.

Logically, I know I look fine. Logically, I know my husband finds me beautiful. Logically, I know that no one who likes (or doesn't like) me does so because of what I look like. When I look at women who look like me or are even bigger than me, I think they look beautiful. Body dysmorphia is very personal. You can think everyone else looks great while thinking you look huge. It is kind of like looking at the grass and seeing blue when everyone else sees green.

I realize this sounds superficial and shallow, but it is so much more than that. I blame the media, ultimately. They do a fantastic job of telling women everywhere what beautiful looks like. And when you are an acne faced teenager who doesn't get asked to prom, you believe these messages. And when you are a 43-year-old woman, those messages still resonate. Maybe even more because now that I am getting older, I have reached the peak of the mountain and am now on the descent about to enter the 'you look good for your age' category. The challenge will be life-long for me. Chemo bloating did not help. At the same time, it did force me to face it head-on. To that end, there is hope that maybe I will begin to place more importance on who I am rather than what I look like.

I don't think there is a woman in America who cannot relate to some extent. I also think there are plenty of men who understand. The media tells us that it is better to be skinny than healthy. They tell women that beautiful is white skin, blonde hair, and blue eyes. There are all sorts of culturally insensitive messages that the media shares with us. I have always fit into the mold of what mainstream media decides is pretty. It's not until now that I got a VERY small glimpse (like the size of a gnat glimpse) of what it must feel like to all those cultures that have never fit that mold.

How sad is it that we cannot embrace a wider description of beauty. But this touches a topic far greater than what I am writing about here. At the end of the day, 'they' tell us that beauty comes from within and that we shouldn't judge a book by its cover. But that doesn't really feel true because it seems like those same people also tell us that no one will read the chapters if the cover is not enticing.

Chapter 17

The Fashion Dilemmas of
Wearing a Scarf

The hardest part about getting ready in the morning was finding a scarf to wear and then figuring out how not to look like a tool while wearing it. I had a lot of very beautiful scarves gifted to me, but I found that I could only wear them when I was wearing solid colors because I had not yet figured out how to match patterns. So the moral of that story is that I needed solid colored scarves.

I also found that material other than silk works best because it doesn't lie as flat on the head. Silk is the prettiest of all the scarves, but also the hardest to make look good on a flat head. My personal favorite is a simple bandanna. Whatever those are made of allow for some volume on the top and side of my head, which balances out the pumpkin shape. So the moral of that story is to get head coverings with a stiffer material.

When people first started seeing me in scarves, someone I know (without knowing it I'm sure) gave me the pity eye and the side-eye. You know, the one where you let out a long breath while saying hello, and the word lingers in the air. I realized at that point that a scarf without makeup made me look like I was sick. So the moral of that story is that I gotta wear some makeup while wearing a headscarf.

If I could walk around with sunglasses on all the time, I would have been all set. Big sunglasses and a headscarf make you look like a movie star who is trying to hide from the public. Without the sunglasses, you look like a cancer patient. Cancer patients are cool and all, but I didn't want the label, so I would have preferred not to look like one. So the moral of that story is that there is no moral. A scarf is going to make you look different. It sucks.

You would think that having no hair would cut down the getting ready time in the morning. Not for me. What happened is that I would spend about 25 minutes trying to match my scarf to my outfit, then another 20 trying to figure out how to wear it. The YouTube videos are overwhelming, so I only really knew a couple of ways to tie a scarf. I was not really thrilled with my look. Apparently, you can have a bad scarf day just like you can have a bad hair day. So the moral of that story is to not assume that because you have no hair that it will take less time to get ready.

I'm not sure what the overall moral of any of this is, really. The terrain is bumpy and there are potholes everywhere. I'm stuck at a never-ending stoplight. My cruise control is broken and my brakes don't work. Cancer sucks. You put on your happy face and 'can do' attitude because you have to and because that is what you are expected to do. But the internal fear is what we don't talk about. The fear that this will not really be over when it is medically over. The fear that it will resurface. The fear that we are not as strong as people say we are. The fear that our old normal is a thing of the past, taken before we were ready to say goodbye. But right then, my biggest fear was that I would never successfully be able to tie a headscarf.

Chapter 18
Round 3 of Chemo

My third round of chemo. This marked the halfway point for me. Three down, three to go. One of the medical professionals who took my blood and read my vitals was very pleasant, which also marked a milestone for me. Her name was Mila, and she was pleasant and calming. My appointment was at 8 AM, so perhaps everyone is just way more pleasant and calming when you are the first person that they see. But I took it as a win.

I told my doctor that my symptoms last time were way worse than the first round and that I didn't get the steroids. Apparently, I should have gotten the steroid pills. The funny thing is, as I was checking out, I had to remind them that I needed the steroid pills. I really hated having to do this. It made me wonder what other medical plan I should've been aware of that I needed to remind them to do. People kept telling me that I needed to advocate, but I hated the thought of that. In this particular situation, advocating seemed to mean I needed to remind people of what they were supposed to do in the first place. I didn't want to do research to know what questions to ask. I wanted the doctors to be thorough enough so that I didn't have to ask the questions.

For round three, the chemo lounge was filled with unfamiliar faces. I was happy to see that most had a support person there with them. In the past, Joe had been the only (or one of two) partner who was there. When I fell off into a Benadryl induced coma, there were a few other people there. I woke up to what felt like happy hour at a local bar. There was chatter, laughter, and everyone being infused with their own special cocktail. Apparently, the chemo party arrived at about 10 AM. Modesty seemed to go out the window in this place as well, with one woman openly farting and then loudly proclaiming to the rest of us that she was sorry, but she ate some really gassy food.

The whole process that time lasted about four hours. This is because I think they misjudged the amount of IV bags I needed. There was one filled with liquid that had been hanging there untouched. Joe had to ask them if they were going to use it. It was then that we realized that having a support person with you is important, not only for emotional support, but to ask all the questions, because the person getting chemo is drowsy and out of it.

I wanted to change my chemo date for round four and five because keeping it where it was meant that round four would interfere with my neighborhood Olympics that we do every first weekend in August, and round five would interfere with a cousin's weekend that had been planned forever. The doctor wouldn't let me make the change. Joe seemed to think it was more important that I didn't mess with the chemo schedule than it was that I attend these events. Apparently, holding off a full week could affect the treatment outcome.

This is exactly what I didn't want to happen when I got diagnosed. I didn't want my life to change. At that point, cancer had taken my hair, my identity, my ability to be as active as I wanted to be. And now it was threatening to take two things from me that I really wanted to do. My only hope was that my side effects went back to how they were after the first round, which would mean that I could still engage in these events. But given that I spent 30 minutes in the bathroom the day after chemo, it appeared that they might be worse.

I felt really sad and frustrated. I hated not being able to control what should be such simple things. I knew I should put on a happy face and tell everyone how great I was doing, but the fact is that it sucked. Cancer sucks. Chemo sucks. Losing my hair sucks. All the side effects suck. Just as I felt I was rounding a corner, I had to go do another round. I lived by 'at leasts'. *At least* it is only bad for a few days, *at least* this will be over in a few months, *at least* my side effects aren't as bad as others, *at least* I don't have to spend a bunch of money on my hair now. The phrase 'at least' is meant to put things into perspective, but it also minimizes the experience. By saying it, maybe I was trying to make it sound like it is not so bad. But it is so bad. It is not terminal, it is not as bad as other people have had, but it is the worst cancer *I* have ever had, and I hated it.

You know what else I hated? Water. I mean, I know water is supposed to taste like nothing, but what it came to taste like to me was like swallowing liquid metal. Everything tasted like metal. Therefore, everything was gross. I tried lemons, I tried cucumbers. I tried all the things you are supposed to try to flavor up water. None of these things overpowered the metal taste. So I just stopped drinking. Subsequently, the doctor told me that I was dehydrated and anemic, and I needed more vitamins and water. So I bought some Vitamin Water. I felt like this kills two birds. No? Whatever. Water sucked. I choked down 90 ounces a day, and it was probably still not enough. This was probably what contributed to my headaches too. Apparently, I also had low blood pressure, which was probably one of the reasons I was tired all the time. That, and the massive amounts of toxins that were entering my body every three weeks.

I spoke with some woman who went through this a few years back. She told me all about what happens after chemo, which scared the shit out of me. This is why I highly advise not thinking too far in advance. I was in the chemo world right then. When I closed that chapter, I would move on to the next. I know some people think it is comforting to know what is coming. Typically, I am that person too, but with this, I was not. To me, it is like telling a first grader what they will be expected to know in fourth grade. They will get there when they get there. Telling them now will only scare them and perhaps cause them not to focus on what they are learning in first grade. I was in first grade. I wanted to focus on first grade right then. And right then, what I knew was that water sucked.

Chapter 19

The Water Struggle is Real

Three days post-chemo, I felt pretty good. When I felt that good, I would tell people I was at about a 95%. For me, that meant that I had some minor stomach issues and some fatigue, but nothing that stopped me from getting on with my normal activities. If I wasn't going through chemo, I would probably rate this same feeling at about an 80%. For me, I think that the first seven or so days after chemo can be equated to going to work with a semi-bad cold. You are not sick enough to stay home, but just don't totally feel like yourself. At the same time, you're not going to walk around and tell all of your coworkers you don't feel well because that's just like putting a sign on your back that says "feel sorry for me, I have a cold."

In any case, I was thankful that round three did not hit me as hard as round two. I could have been putting the cart before the horse, as I still had about five days before I could declare victory, but this felt more like the first time than the last time. It was probably the loss of the steroid pills from the last round that made me have the reactions I did. It was the only thing that has changed. My public service announcement is this: If you are going through chemo, make sure that you are provided with ALL the medication before you leave treatment.

So let's get back to the water for a minute. I was winning. I had been successful in drinking 100 fluid ounces of water a day. I forced myself to scarf down actual water before I moved on to Vitamin Water, which offers more flavor. Who would have thought that my days would consist of counting the fluid ounces of water I take in a day? If only it were this hard to drink wine.

Chapter 20
This Shit is Hard

I need to take a minute to talk about something other than physical symptoms. I want to talk about the things that people don't talk about. Most cancer patients walk around with their heads held high, trying desperately to portray an air of confidence and 'I'm fine' attitude. But what we don't tell you is that we are really a mess inside. This shit is hard.

The mental strain of cancer is sometimes worse than the physical strain. You know that phrase, "You are stronger than you think?" What are those words supposed to mean? So as my stomach is in knots and I'm locked in the bathroom, and I have to tell my son that I cannot play with him right now because I am too tired, those words are supposed to jolt me into a reality that says "Hold on, Monica. You forgot. You are stronger than you think." Those words don't make my stomach feel better or suddenly give me the energy of a three-year-old. I kind of thought I was pretty strong before this happened. But being thrown against a wall by a 1000-ton force promises to break the strongest of people.

The fatigue is no joke either. At least for the seven days after a treatment, I didn't ever feel rested. I had no energy or strength. I forced myself to eat spoonfuls of peanut butter because I needed the protein. I found myself wishing for rain because then at least there was an excuse to stay in. Sunny days made me feel guilty because I didn't feel well enough to get out and enjoy it. There are things I wanted to do with Jacob, but then I'd wake up, and it was all I could do to get him to and from activities in the morning. My temper was short because I was hangry. I couldn't eat anything without immediately experiencing raging diarrhea, so I was constantly irritable.

The poor kid got the worst of me. Some days, I would put him in camp so I could rest. In my mind, I would think of all the things I should do around the house, but 30 minutes into it, I had to sit down. I have wonderful people around me that would take him for a while, and he has great friends in the neighborhood that he can play with. But none of that erased the guilt I felt because I didn't get to be the one making the memories with him this summer. I know that this was temporary, but being eight years old is temporary too. What if this was how he would remember me?

Let me walk you through a typical morning the week after chemo. This is not pretty, but it is real. I get up in the morning, force myself to exercise because I know I need it for my mental well-being. Then I take a shower. Then I spend the next 30 minutes breaking out in cold sweats and going in and out of the bathroom. During this week, when Jacob is taking tennis, I have equal amounts of anxiety because I am not sure I will be able to leave the bathroom to get him to his lessons on time. Jacob then asks if I am okay because he is worried. Then he tells me that he is sorry that I don't feel well. When we get back from tennis, I want to eat, so I try. That doesn't go well. I am immediately back in the bathroom for another 30 minutes. So I stop eating. I drink water. All day. I hate the water. I try to do one element of housework a day. Yesterday, it was laundry. I will take my dog for a walk because it is good to get outside. I am exhausted when I get back. This process continues for the next seven days.

I read somewhere that chemo can cause cold-like symptoms. So on top of feeling gross because of poisons, I also got to enjoy a summer cold. My eyes were in a constant state of watering, making it look like I was crying all the time. My nose ran and my head was stuffed. I remember getting this feeling last time but figured that it was indeed a summer cold. After experiencing it again, I dug a little deeper and found that this is one of the many side effects that I might experience.

Turns out that chemo over time causes a body to feel tired the more and more treatments are given. I don't feel so tired that I can't move, but I do tend to get pretty exhausted in the middle of the day. Oftentimes, a 20-minute nap would do the trick. Sometimes, I needed more. I have taken Dayquil on more than one occasion because it combats the cold-like symptoms, and in turn, also helps me feel awake. I realize that this was probably a bad choice, but a girl's gotta wake up. I had to do summer.

I had a love/hate with the few days before my next treatment. I typically felt the best in the two days leading up to it. It was bittersweet because I knew that my time of feeling good was about to be traded in for time alternating between bed, couch, and bathroom, along with generally feeling guilty because I couldn't do much else. I also knew my taste buds would disappear for a while, and I would be left staring at the peanut butter chocolate ice cream in my fridge, craving a bowl but not being able to have any because it would upset my stomach. I had to remember to protein up this time, and ice cream was probably not the best way to do that. Also, the damn water. I would have to be very aware of drinking a ton of water again because my body would inevitably become dehydrated due to all the trips I took to the bathroom.

*

That summer had been punctuated by vomiting, fatigue, diarrhea, sore throat, and headaches. On the peripheral lies the beach, time with friends, wine nights, and bonfires. I wish it were the other way around.

Oh, and the wonderful acid reflux that gives me the sensation of fire coming up through my throat, tickling my gag reflexes. This is the best. Am I going to puke? Is my throat going to erupt in flames? You just don't know. The mystery is what keeps it exciting.

If a person could die from acid reflux, I might have been in jeopardy of expiring soon. I used to think that I had this before, but I have learned that saying that you have acid reflux when you just have heartburn is like having a bad headache and declaring it a migraine. A migraine is debilitating to the point where you cannot open your eyes. A bad headache hurts like a mother, but you can still walk around. Acid reflux is a semi-truck. Heartburn is a big wheel.

Acid reflux is way more painful than I thought it would be. It almost entices vomiting at times. You know those people who put fire in their throat? Well, this is the opposite. Fire was actually coming *out* of my throat from the depth of my esophagus. It's like lava erupting. I heard apple cider vinegar helps with this, so I tried it. That was a bad choice. I took a tablespoon of it and immediately felt like flaming pieces of glass were running down my throat. The word 'vinegar' should have tipped me off, but I am a little slow on the uptake.

Also, I still had the mild feeling of Novocain on my lips and tongue. It is a bizarre feeling because I constantly had low-grade numbness. I tried a protein shake. Tasted like sandpaper. But at least I finally got some protein and calories in my system. I had been in an abusive relationship with my stomach. I had treated it with kid gloves and had let nothing toxic enter it for way longer than I would like, but nothing made the bitch happy.

So reactions from chemo to chemo are unpredictable. The first time was super manageable. The second time was miserable but only lasted for about three days. The third time the side effects were not nearly as bad as the time before but lasted for way longer. I also had cravings that I didn't have before. I suddenly really wanted a pile of buffalo French fries from Kickstand, which is a local bar where I live. That and a martini. I really wanted a dirty martini with four blue cheese stuffed olives.

Chapter 21
Hello, Martini, My Old Friend

Something about day eight makes me snap back into the land of the living and feel functional again. I relish the two weeks that I have of feeling normal before I have to have another treatment, and I find that I tried to pack three weeks' worth of activity into this time frame.

My body tired quicker than it used to, but I tried to will myself into having the same energy level that I did before cancer. Oftentimes, just going outside and getting some vitamin D does the trick. Perhaps it was fortunate that chemo happened in the summer when there tends to be ample supplies of it. Radiation would happen in the winter when it tends to be darker. But I decided to cross that bridge when I come to it.

I was able to enjoy a martini for the first time, which was euphoric to me. Also, coffee. Which tasted like liquid heaven. And FOOD! I could eat again. I've had French fries and ice cream with hot fudge. Neither are the ideal diet of a cancer patient, but when you go a full week of eating almost nothing, all you want to do is stuff your face with all the things that are the least healthy.

My morning exercise routines had become less taxing, and I was able to hit the tennis ball around the courts for a while. Sure, I got winded easily, but it felt exhilarating nonetheless. If I could just get those head coverings to look like they were an intentional part of my outfit, my world would be at peace again.

Chapter 22

Is This Normal? Am I Normal?

The day before chemo was becoming more daunting than the day after. It had come to the point that I knew well enough what to expect. Knowing what was going to happen to my body, my mind, and my spirit, and not being able to do anything about it felt helpless and scary. It felt like I was walking the plank and the chemo chair was the shark-infested waters. When you fall, you know there are sharks beneath you. With each treatment, I was left to wonder if I would be bitten by one shark or many. But I knew I would be bitten, and the number of sharks that got me would determine the severity of my wounds.

I started to have more emotionally rough days leading up to the next treatment. It had been annoying because I felt so good physically. But what they don't tell you is how this would affect you emotionally. Even after you lose all your hair. Even after you know what each chemo reaction will bring. Even after all of your friends and family have seen your new normal and have embraced it. They don't tell you that you will have moments of anger so strong, you don't know if you will be able to overcome them. They don't tell you that you will break down in spontaneous tears and not be able to site a viable reason. They don't tell you that you will still look at yourself in the mirror and think yourself ugly, because cancer has not only taken your hair, but has left you with dark circles under your eyes and discolored skin. They don't tell you that you will see your friends living their life and get jealous that you cannot live yours in the way you want to right now.

I felt like a fraud before cancer. Turns out that I still felt like I was going to get found out. But this time, instead of people finding out that I'm stupid, people would find out that I am weak. If they saw the tears, if they experienced the anger, they would know that my exterior is a front meant to mask the fear that lies beneath.

The thing is, I don't think that I am abnormal in any of this. I think that most people who are going through cancer, or really anything that knocks them off their feet, feel this way. I wish we would see advertisements of people who would help us all feel normal. I see survivors, but I don't see people who are still in the trenches. If I had the ability, I would make such a commercial so that people would know they are not alone. I would talk about how feeling weak does not mean you are not strong, how it's okay to want to punch walls sometimes and scream at the top of your lungs.

I would talk about how it is hard to say goodbye to the version of who you were and it is okay to mourn that person. It is scary to not know what all of these medications and treatments are going to do to your body. They will take away the cancer, but what will they leave in their wake?

Chapter 23

Stories from the Chair

It's funny the things that you notice in the chemo chair over time. Sitting in the chair for the fourth time, feeling my eyes get heavy, and eventually closing with the weight of Benadryl, I listened to the sounds around me. I noticed that having my eyes closed helped me hear. Getting rid of one sense really does seem to heighten others. I enjoyed listening to the conversations happening around me. This is what I heard:

The older gentleman across from me is talking to the nurse. He seems to be doing chemo and radiation simultaneously, or maybe he did radiation first and is now on to chemo. In any case, he is a retired tool and dye professional. He is explaining to the nurse that radiation has made him more tired than the chemo has. This makes me worried. Can this be possible? If this is true, the worst is yet to come for me. Coupled with the fact that I will be at work when I am experiencing radiation, the fatigue will be even worse to deal with. Students and parents don't care if you're tired.

There is another pair talking about politics. Something about insurance premiums. The conversation is one that I have listened to, or had, too many times to count, so I am bored listening to it again and move on.

A woman is telling a man that the aliens are taking over the government. I thought she was on the train to crazy town until I realized that she was talking about a movie where this happened. Had my eyes been opened, I may not have listened to that part and thought that she might be in the wrong type of hospital.

Then there's the couple talking about hair. One has a full head of hair. He said that chemo never took that from him. I wanted to secretly punch him in the face. The woman's hair was taken from her and she is complaining that her scalp hurts. The man then says that we are about 10 degrees colder without hair, but I wonder how he knows this because he has hair. I swear, it is always the people who have not had the experience that have the most to say. Meanwhile, I have hot flashes, so this is not true for me.

There is a woman who is talking to someone about how she chose to wear a wig because she works in business as a trainer and a headscarf is distracting to people. I say, F that. Wear your headscarf, acknowledge you are wearing one, and move on. It is only the elephant in the room when you don't address it. But still, I get it. I thought about wearing a wig too. Sometimes it is just easier not to have to constantly explain yourself.

The most annoying is the loud conversation of the four people who have chosen to sit in the private room (there is a private room for those who elect to wear an ice cap or whatever it is called so they can keep their hair. I guess when you have ice on your head for eight hours, you deserve to have a little privacy). There is a door to the private room. One you can shut. They have elected to leave it open and have a party so that we are all privy to their inside jokes and laughter.

This motley crew of chemo patients entertained me until I finally fell off to sleep. But I did learn a lesson; if you want to be a good listener, keep your eyes shut.

Chapter 24
Reading is Detrimental

My stomach hurt. It kept me up all night with piercing pain. Also, I walked up the stairs and nearly hyperventilated. I thought I might pass out. Who knew it would be so treacherous to walk from one side of the house to the other. Still, I felt like I reacted decently to that round of chemo. If the stomach pangs went away, I would feel fine.

Also, my eyesight had gotten worse. I had to wear readers on top of my contacts on a consistent basis in order for the written word to be legible. That could've been my age, but I'm blaming chemo. I could only hope my sight returned to normal after chemo.

Speaking of after chemo. I read on some blogs that a lot of people lose their lashes and eyebrows after the last treatment. This is why I don't read. Reading is not fundamental; it is detrimental. Now instead of thinking I got lucky by keeping them, I was convinced that my lashes would disappear. Unlike the decision to have a bald head and not wear a wig, I would not have bald eyes. There would be synthetically enhanced lashes in my future if that happened.

You would think I would have lost some of my vanity by then, but I hadn't. I think it is the one thing I was still trying to control in that mess. In a sea of chaos, you cling to what you know. That's true of anything. When tragedy strikes, we search for explanations that make sense to us when nothing else does, even if those explanations are not planted in reality.

There were days when I didn't feel like I was emotionally going to get through this. These days were pretty predictable because they were always the first week after treatment. There were days when I wanted to scream about how unfair this was. There were days when I cried all day. I knew I would get through it because there were no options other than to keep moving. My ability to persevere would not be rooted in the fact that I am stronger than I think. Instead, it will be rooted in the fact that I think that I am strong. And therein lies the difference.

Chapter 25

The Story of the Prosthetic Leg

My cancer journey started in May. It was August now. Summer. I love the summer. Lazy days, sunshine, going to the beach, swimming.

Swimming is my favorite of all exercises. I love the water, especially pool water. There is something about it that is so serene and therapeutic to me. When I am swimming, all I can hear is the sound of the water, and I am in my own world.

My in-laws belong to a swim club. Sometimes they invite us to join them for a day of relaxation and fun. This summer was no exception, except that I was so insecure about my bald head.

Losing my hair and feeling like I am being stared at is one thing, but how would I swim without a cap on my head? I was so nervous and resorted to sitting poolside watching everyone else have fun.

On our way there, our car pulled up alongside a woman with a bald head driving her SUV. Women don't shave their heads unless they are a badass or a cancer patient, so I figured she must be one or the other. And if she is a cancer patient, she is automatically a badass.

I was envious of her ability to own who she is. Joe asked if I would ever want to do that, and I said that I wish that I had the courage. It is so inspiring to me to see women who own everything about who they are because it is something I have always struggled with.

When we got to the swim club, Jacob ran straight to the pool while I watched him jumping off the diving board, sliding down the slide, and having a generally good time. At one point I went in to join him, and we had a great time splashing around. But I stayed where the water was only waist-high.

Every hour, the club announces an adults-only swim. All the kids have to get out so that the adults can have the pool to themselves for 15 minutes. About 10 minutes after I got into the pool to play with Jacob, this was called. So Jacob got out, but I decided to stay in and enjoy the water.

I was enjoying doing the breaststroke and side stroke from end to end of the pool, but they have never been my favorite strokes. I like freestyle, and I love to submerge myself in the water. My father-in-law must have sensed this desire because at one point, he swam slowly over to me and said "You know, I have this friend who only has one leg. One time a few of us went to a pool and he just took his prosthetic off, right there in front of everyone and got in the pool. He said it was the best feeling he has ever felt. That prosthetic never really fit just right. But without it, he could float."

There was a lot of wisdom in that story. I am sure that my father-in-law was trying to tell me that sometimes we need to let go of the things that give us security so we can lean into the freedom that uncertainty brings.

So behind my tear-filled sunglasses, I untied my head covering, took off my glasses, and fell deep into the water. I swam freestyle. I immersed myself into the deepest part of the pool, and it was wonderful. The water cascading off of my bald head felt like fear escaping my body. I didn't look around me as I unveiled my new look. I didn't want to risk seeing people stare at me. This wasn't about them. This was about me finding the courage to do something I never thought that I would do. I felt free. I felt liberated and empowered. And when I did take the time to look around, no one was staring at me. At least not in the point your finger, look at her kind of way.

I kept my scarf off of my head for a few hours after that, until it got cold and I had to put it back on. I didn't know if I would do something like that again, but I did it once, and it felt like climbing Everest. Like the prosthetic leg, my scarves never seemed to fit just right. Taking it off allowed me to float.

Chapter 26
The Day of Reckoning

Like many things, just when you get used to a new normal, the earth erupts and shakes up your insecurities just to make sure you are paying attention.

The summer was full of firsts. My first chemo, my first day without hair, my first swim in a pool without a head covering. Now comes another first. My first day back at work.

I return to work a week before teachers do and two weeks before students. I should have been happy that I had the opportunity to ease my way into this new world of Mrs. Fugedi, the cancer patient.

Instead of feeling any amount of gratefulness, I felt an immense sense of anxiety. When the students left in June, I had hair, and when they returned I would not. Thankfully, the staff knew all about what was going on. Many had seen my new look, so I would feel some comfort walking into the support that they had already shown me. But the parents and students. That made me scared and confused about how to handle this most awkward event.

It's not like I work in an office building where there are a finite number of people. You tell them, and it is over. In a school, it is ongoing. There are close to 1300 students, plus one or two parents for each. It is harder to keep your personal life private. And many students do not yet have the capacity to know that this is a personal topic and are unfiltered in their response. I didn't want to have to explain one-on-one to every person who enters my office that I have cancer, and then open myself up to all the questioning that follows. They do not know, nor do some of them care, that my emotions are on my sleeve and every question they ask might elicit tears.

The only way I know how to handle stressful situations is with humor. I was sure that I would say something really sarcastic and inappropriate just to deflect. Something like "It's just cancer. It's not like it can kill you." Many people already look at me strangely because my humor is too dry for them. A comment like that would leave them wildly confused.

But seriously. What was I supposed to do? Send a letter to my entire caseload letting them know that the pink elephant had entered the building? That seemed a bit much and really pretentious to think that my cancer warrants a newsletter. Perhaps I should put a sign on my door that reads "I have cancer, but don't worry, I will still be able to complete your college applications." No, that seemed rude too. Although let's be honest, many of my seniors and their parents would be worried about this.

I figured I would probably only have to tell one or two people and just let them spread it through the grapevine. Although we know how the grapevine goes. By the time it gets back to me, I will have stage 4 lung cancer and have six months to live. This is the one case where I was kind of hoping people would talk behind my back. Perhaps some students would ask a teacher, and the teacher would tell them. Or maybe they would ask another counselor and hear it that way.

In any case, I decided that I probably wouldn't say anything at all and hope it all just went away. That would totally happen, right?

It turns out going back to work proved a far more vulnerable experience than I had thought. I had hoped that by wearing a headscarf all summer I would be emotionally ready to handle any questions, stares, or comments that I would get. Apparently not.

I had a new principal at the high school I work at. She knew all about the cancer because the grapevine has a way of spreading information, which is fine because honestly, that's how I preferred people to find out. Still, I thought it would be appropriate if she heard my story from the person who is writing it, so I scheduled a meeting with her.

My intent was to talk all about the role of a high school counselor and only spend a minute on the treatment I would have that year. I started off talking about the cancer. I figured we had a big pink elephant in the room, and I should address that first before moving on to something else. That was stupid.

I started off with "I know you know I have cancer," and then went on to tell her that I had about 90 sick days banked because I never take time off, and that I had spent eleven years trying to demonstrate a really good work ethic, and how all this comes into play because the person she may see this year may not be the person that I spent eleven years trying to create. I should have stopped there. That was solid. But I didn't. Mostly because I'm stupid.

I started talking about my chemo treatments. That was fine. But then I went on to talk about what comes after my chemo treatments. The surgery, the radiation. All of this would pretty much take me through the year. And I started to cry. Like, really cry. I tried to deflect by backtracking to talk about a high school counselor, but now I sounded like a babbling moron who was trying to piece together words that made no sense. So now I had given the impression that I was not only weak, but that I was also scattered. Neither of which are true (well, sometimes I'm scattered).

So that was my conversation with my principal. Then people started coming to my office. People whom I really like. They came to ask me how I was doing, and I was happy to tell them. So I would tell them, they would leave, and I would find myself crying again. What was wrong with me? You would think I have cancer or something.

At one point, Lezah, one of my close friends and coworkers, noticed the blank look I had on my face and asked me how I was doing. Not "How are you doing with the cancer," but "How are you doing back in this environment?" And again, I started to cry.

I was not doing well. This was so much harder than I anticipated. I thought that I could hide behind my mask of humor and nonchalant attitude. I would deflect when people asked, and I would do everything I could to help everyone else feel comfortable with my cancer.

That never works, and it didn't work that time either. The best way I know how to describe it is that I felt like my insides were on my outside. Completely exposed, unable to hide. And ugly. Don't forget ugly. I mean, when your intestines are sitting on the outside of your body, it is not pretty.

And let's not forget that pretty is who I was. It was the *only* thing I knew how to be. Without a pretty veil to hide behind, I felt stupid and worthless. I have a friend who lost their hair because of chemo and didn't have a second thought about it. I envy her strength and her ability to not define herself by what she looked like.

Me? Not so lucky. I never had to entertain the thought that I could be anything but pretty. Because of that, I never investigated any other quality I might have. It was about my appearance, and my hair played the leading role.

So as students trickled into my office, they would look at me oddly as if to say, "Tell me about this headscarf you got going on." But they wouldn't ask because it's weird. I mean, would you ask? I wouldn't. Equally, I wouldn't tell them. So we just sat there in my office, the pink elephant becoming ever more prominent. I'm so good at handling personally vulnerable situations. I mean really, I'm quite awesome at it…if awesome means sucky.

On two occasions, I had parents tell me that they assumed I was trying a new fashion because "you are always so fashionable." While I appreciate this compliment, *really?* You really thought I was trying to put a scarf on my head and seeing if it picks up steam with the general population?

I know that vulnerability breeds human connection. I also know that privacy is important to me. But I had cancer. I lost my hair, and therefore also lost my privacy. I wasn't sure how I was going to manage being vulnerable while still having a sense of privacy.

So the first week back at work was harder than I thought. When I think about it, my emotions were spawned through the retelling of my story. I have compartmentalized my treatments to preserve my sanity. At that time, I was in chemo. I had not given much thought to life after chemo. So when I was telling my principal about the entirety of my treatment and all the shit I had to go through this year, it made me think "I have a lot of shit to go through this year." Saying it out loud made it real, and maybe there was still a part of me that wasn't ready for it to be real. I can only take reality in chunks. I don't want it all at the same time.

Thankfully, reality came at me slowly. I was about to go into my next chemotherapy treatment. That meant for a little while, I didn't have to think about how I was going to handle the back to school madness. So thank you, chemo.

I guess.

Chapter 27
Chemo: Round 5

I had to go to a different location for that session of chemotherapy because I changed the date from Thursdays to Mondays, and my doctor only works out of a different hospital on Mondays. I didn't think that would be a big deal, but there were definitely some differences in the two locations. But there were also some similarities.

Let's start with the similarities.

First, it appeared the people who take your vitals all take training in impersonal behavior. I didn't want to be an inconvenience or anything, but I was kinda about to have chemo. Perhaps I was a little scared. When scared, I might ask questions that seem obvious or annoying to you. Please just bear with me. I am about to walk down the green mile to await my poisoning.

Also, doctors are interesting creatures. I loved my oncologist, but when he is done talking, he expected me to know what my next steps were. When we were done with my consultation (they do this before sending you into the den of sickness), he simply walked out of the office. I had never been to that place, so I didn't know where the chemo room was. Thankfully, there was a nice nurse who noticed the look of irritation and confusion on my face and showed me the way.

When I got there, I had to wait in line for the next available chair. This nice woman, who was there with her father, assured me that it was not always this backed up. I always appreciated those people who notice when someone is on edge and try to calm them. I hope I can be one of those people.

Once I got settled, I had time to look around and observe. This has been something I have increasingly enjoyed doing. People watching has always been a fascinating phenomenon.

The first thing I noticed was a girl walking past me with a cold cap on. This is what you use if you want to keep your hair. She looked like an alien, and all I could think of was that she had to be there for eight hours instead of four with a freezing cold ice pack on her head. All for a 70% chance of keeping 80% of her hair. Also, when you think about it, if you lose your hair you can blame your bitchiness on your cancer. Visible illnesses are so much more effective then invisible illnesses.

Then there was this chatty Cathy nurse who refused to use her inside voice. SHUT THE FUCK UP! Don't you know I have cancer? And to add insult to injury, she spoke like a preschool teacher, so now I hated her. And someone just said 'bitch' to describe his female dog and was being serious. Have you ever heard someone use that term correctly out loud?

This is everything I noticed before Benadryl kicked in. Ah! Benadryl. Chemo is one of the only places you can go where you can legally get high and then pass out for three hours.

When I did wake up from my drug-induced slumber, I had more observations. Thoughts seem to flow smoothly when you have nothing else to do. You become really observant. I came up with an invention about garage door openers. I decided that they should make cars with a chip built-in that recognizes their garage. That way, when your car pulls up, your garage automatically opens and you never have to worry about losing your garage door opener again. If you are reading this and decide to invent such a device, please give me some compensation for the idea.

So that was my 5th chemo experience. I had one more to go.

Chapter 28
Five Days Later

Day five post-chemo was definitely the worst day for me. No matter if my reactions were mild or severe, day five always seemed to be worse than others. I just felt so tired. My limbs and my entire face were numb. My stomach was in knots, and that damn metal taste prevented me from enjoying some really good food.

During this whole experience, I felt really guilty because I saw Joe having to take on the brunt of what seemed like everything during the week post-chemo. He didn't complain, which only made me feel like a slacker.

In my overly analytical, insecure head, I felt like people would think I was faking being sick. Isn't that stupid? Who was going to think I was faking feeling bad because I had cancer? Maybe it's because one day I felt totally fine and then the next, totally not fine.

August is a beautiful month in Michigan. I don't think the summer of 2017 was any different, but I wouldn't know because I spent so much time on the couch. One by one, all the beautiful days were wasting away.

I was determined to do something for the household, so I managed to get to the grocery store. I found myself next to a woman in the cheese aisle who wore a red bandanna. I could see that her hair was growing back, but that she must not yet be comfortable going without head coverings. She was probably about my age. As we were both grabbing a block of provolone, our eyes met.

There is nothing so profound to me as when two strangers have an unspoken connection. We smiled at each other as if to say "Yep, I get it," and then went on our way. No words were spoken, but so much was said.

It was in these small moments that I found some sense of reassurance. When I felt at my worst, when all I wanted to do was retreat from the world and cry over my own self-pity, I was reminded that I am not the only person fighting this battle. I am only one part of a tribe of women (and some men) who all share a small piece of the story. My piece of the puzzle does not make the design, but it adds the colors. I just hope that my strokes are broad enough for people to see.

Chapter 29

There Goes My Eyesight...Kinda

Well, there goes my eyesight. I mean, I wasn't going blind or anything, but my eyesight seemed significantly compromised. Contacts now only offered blurred vision. I had to wear readers on top of my contacts. And not the +1.0 readers that I typically have to use simply because I am now over 40, but +1.75. And even then I am straining to see.

I asked my doctor about this when I saw him last. He said I should make an appointment with my eye doctor. But then I asked him if my eyesight would return to normal when chemo was finished. He said it would, then proceeded to tell me if the eye doctor gave me a new prescription, don't fill it because I won't be able to see once my vision returns to where it was.

So, let me get this straight. My vision is worse because of chemo. When chemo is finished, my vision will be back to where it was. I should make an appointment with the eye doctor, but don't fill a prescription. Wait. What? So what is the point? Shouldn't I just wait it out then? I had one more chemo left. I'd managed that far not to crash or walk into anything.

So anyway, aside from the hijacking of my optical proficiency, my reactions so far had remained pretty status quo. Metal mouth, fatigue, no taste buds, digestive issues. You know, the normal.

Chapter 30

Paint with Broad Strokes

The thing about only reading one chapter at a time is that you risk a surprise ending. Rolling with the punches is not something I do well. But I suppose I set myself up when I decided to compartmentalize cancer.

About a day after the last chemo, I got a call from the surgeon to schedule a consultation appointment for the next step. So I guess that meant my first chapter was nearing an end, and I had to prepare myself for the next.

My appointment was at 2:20. They told me to be there 30 minutes prior. I'm unclear as to why this was so important given that I waited for over an hour and a half to see the doctor. At one point, a commercial for Olga's came on. I love Olga's. Their curly fries, gyro, salad, and snackers. It truly is one of the best places on earth. Or perhaps it just felt that way because at 3:30 the day before, my body decided to regain its appetite. We were in the waiting room long enough to get an intermission to go get something to eat, so I settled for grabbing a lemon pound cake from the Starbucks in the hospital lobby. It was fantastic.

The surgeon's personality entered the room before she did. She was down to earth, funny, and had exceptionally beautiful hair. I found this ironic. I immediately liked her. Because Joe and I only know how to inappropriately joke when we are nervous, when we introduced ourselves, he said something snarky about me, and I introduced him as my first husband. For a split second, I think we were all confused as to whether we were there to talk about cancer or meet up for happy hour. We decided cancer would be a more appropriate topic given our venue.

The surgeon didn't know that my oncologist had not yet told me in detail about anything that would be happening after chemo, so she got to be the poor soul to rip the Band-Aid off. To be clear, I thought I was just there to talk about surgery.

Not so much.

My last chemo was scheduled for September 18th. Surgery had to happen no sooner than October 9th and no later than November 4th. I could choose whether I wanted a lumpectomy or mastectomy. I imagined the decision is as easy as choosing whether I wanted fries with my cheeseburger.

My chances of cancer re-emerging were the same regardless of which path I took, so you would think it would be a no brainer. A lumpectomy is less intrusive. HOWEVER, what I also learned is I would need radiation after surgery. It would be every day for seven weeks. I was told that I would not be able to travel during radiation. So naturally, in my head, I had all these plans to travel to exotic locations between October and December.

I tried negotiating when surgery had to happen and radiation times. Apparently, my preferences did not play a factor in my therapy. I was quickly told I don't get to control this and I just needed to be patient. I don't even understand what that word meant, much less how to practice it.

There was a chance that if I did a mastectomy that I would not need radiation. I was told that I should not base my decision on this, but I felt like I was totally going to base my decision on this. I did NOT want radiation. I mean, it's radiation. Aside from the annoying disturbance to my daily routine and the additional fatigue it would bring, IT IS RADIATION! I feel like that's not good for you in the long term.

I was supposed to meet with a radiation oncologist to find out what the chances of not needing radiation after a mastectomy were. These are decisions I didn't want to make. Sure, I'll get a free boob job, and to some that might sound exciting. I can go from a small to a large. But I've never really cared about my breasts. I mean, they're fine, but I never wanted them bigger or smaller. Too bad breast cancer doesn't require surgery to take away the cellulite on my thighs and ass. I'd totally be excited about that.

So okay, great. Now I knew about surgery and radiation. I was ready to pack up and leave, but the doctor kept talking. There's more. There's more? What the hell? How many pieces of me do you want? So apparently, I was told I would have to see my oncologist twice a year for like, ten years! AND I would need to take pills, perhaps all of my life. PLUS, and here is the kicker, for an entire year, I would have to go back to the chemo place and get injected with one or two of the four drugs that I had been getting all along. I would need to do this for an hour every three weeks for ONE YEAR. 365 days. 525,949.2 minutes.

If they decided to use Pregeta (the diarrhea drug), then I may experience all the digestive issues that I had with chemo—for a year.

When I'm done with the year-long needle tour, I get another year before I am projected to feel normal again. I didn't even know what normal felt like anymore, but I imagined at that point, it would feel like euphoria.

So this is what you get when you make one lousy trip to the doctor. A daunting short-term future and a craving for Olga's.

Chapter 31
Damn Vulnerability

Lots of vulnerable conversations happened over the last few weeks. I felt like I was on an explanation tour. I was constantly having to explain what was happening to students, parents, colleagues, and even strangers.

The conversation didn't get easier the more I talked about it. I always started off strong and ended feeling emotional. Vulnerability is hard. Probably the hardest thing in the world for me. But what I found is that people are good. The ones who care about you rally around you, and you end up finding that there are more people who care than you ever imagined. This in itself made me feel vulnerable, but at the same time made me feel loved. And feeling loved is the most comforting feeling to me.

I figure somewhere in the middle of the hardest and best emotions is where growth happens.

Chapter 32

Swedish Fish Level Stress

You know what I do when I get stressed? I eat gummy candy. This time, I found myself eating a bag of Swedish Fish. I don't like Swedish Fish, but they were there in front of me, so I ate them. You know what I really like? Those chewy Werther Originals. Those are tasty. But none were available in my time of need, so I grabbed the fish.

The day didn't start out in a stressful way. It only escalated to Swedish Fish levels when my phone started ringing off the hook with doctor after doctor calling me about appointments. The last time this happened was the day after I found out I had cancer. It must be a sign that a new chapter is about to begin when the medical professionals start harassing you.

So first the MRI was scheduled. Then the appointment with the radiation oncologist, followed by an appointment with the plastic surgeon. Last was the phone call from the surgeon's office to schedule the follow-up appointment.

All of these phone calls and appointments were made within a one-hour time span. And the doctors did not at all care what my schedule looked like. I didn't get to choose the time or date. Damn cancer thinks it owns me or something.

So I get off the phone, and within minutes, I am talking about how to make the most of your college essay with a student, followed by talking someone down from an anxiety spin, followed by a few more schedule changes, followed by trying to figure out how to manage Google Forms. The good news is that these distractions allowed me to get out of my own head, so I didn't get to process what was going on until the workday was over.

Enter Swedish Fish.

Chapter 33
This Super Sucks

September 18th marked the last day of chemotherapy. It proved to be the most annoying chemo yet. Not because of the poisons pumping into me, but because of the inordinate amount of wait time that I had to endure.

My appointment was at 10:15. I did not sit in a chair until 12:15, and the process lasted over four hours, which is crazy. The fact that doctors overbook patients so that their time is not wasted when and if patients cancel makes me wonder how patient-centered medical professionals really are.

So no one canceled because who is canceling their chemo appointment? It's not like this is a dental cleaning. Miss that and you may get a little extra plaque buildup. Miss chemo, and you may be compromising your health in a way that could affect your life. So because this overbooking situation happened, I had to wait for two hours.

I spent a total of six and a half hours in the hospital for an appointment that should have lasted three and a half. I felt especially bad for my husband who did not get the advantage of sleeping for three hours. Instead, he sat in a very uncomfortable chair and read. I told him he could leave, but he wanted to be there to make sure they didn't miss anything. What a trooper. I probably would have found the closest Starbucks and settled in with a good book. He is a better person than me.

Maybe I was extra ornery because that was my last chemo and I just wanted to get the hell out of there. Or maybe it was because as a school counselor who makes appointments with parents all the time, I would never book double appointments. Maybe the next time I make an appointment with a parent who is also a doctor, I will book another one at the same time and make them wait. Then I will tell them that I surely did not think they would mind because I thought this is the kind of meeting etiquette that doctors liked.

Anyway, enough complaining. I should have just been happy that I was able to get treatment at all. But what fun is cancer if you can't weave in snarky sarcasm and generally bad taste anecdotes every now and again?

The day after my last chemo round, I was gifted with waves of nausea. On top of that, I was so tired that I am sure I could've easily dozed off while a choir of heavy metal '80s bands sung directly into my ear.

I don't know why, but for some reason, I got it in my head that the last chemo would be relatively easy. I figured I'd been through five rounds already and had experienced some pretty bad symptoms. Surely, the Universe would reward me by making this time around bearable. The Universe is a jaded little bitch.

Normally I don't feel the effects of chemo until at least five days afterward. This time, I was feeling it the very next day. I was exhausted the whole day. The fatigue had only been aggravated by a constant pile on of symptoms as each day progressed. By the time day five rolled around, I was exhausted. I had the familiar metal taste in my mouth, the feeling of glass every time I swallowed, stomach issues, and I was numb. My whole body felt like it had been injected with Novocain.

The weekend after my last chemo round, my husband and son went on a camping trip, so I had the house to myself. Usually, I use this time to do something productive. Not this time. This time all I could do was will myself off the couch to go buy some bananas (the lack of potassium and protein that comes from being on a five-day starvation diet causes some pretty bad cramping, particularly in my feet). It was going to be 90 degrees and sunny all weekend. I would not be enjoying any of it.

I don't admit defeat easily, and I don't do excuses. Although it does not pass the out loud test, cancer to me felt like an excuse. I constantly asked myself things like, "Are you cancer-tired or are you just tired and want to blame cancer?" I'm not sure I even knew the difference anymore. But I did know that my body was run down. My mind was tired. I didn't have the sustained energy like I used to, and I worried if I would ever feel awake again.

I tried to take all of this in stride, but there were days when I got pretty bitter. People were far kinder to me than I was to myself. Before leaving for camping, my husband told me to do nothing all weekend. People at work told me that I'm not winning any medals by being there. I've been told that it is okay to take a step back. But it was never about that for me. I was not trying to posture myself in a way that made me look like I was a badass that went to work through

121

cancer. I was not trying to gain praise, sympathy, admiration, or any of that.

All I wanted was to be normal. All I was really trying to have was as normal of a routine as I could. Being present, that's important to me. Success is measured in all different ways. Right then, for me, success was just showing up. So while I knew I didn't HAVE to go to work, I NEEDED to go to work, because if I didn't then the cancer wins, and I was not going to let an eight-ton pink elephant beat me.

Chapter 34
Chemo Light

My chemo was really not over after my last round. Next, I had to move to what I called chemo light. I would not get all the drugs, but I would get at least one, maybe two. Herceptin was a for sure drug. Perjeta was a maybe. The doctor wanted me to do both, but I said no to the Perjeta. Apparently, studies have shown it to be significant in its ability to keep the cancer at bay in only 1% of the population. The doctor wanted the extra 1%, but I wanted control of my bowels, so I decided I would take the risk.

I had to do this chemo light every three weeks for ONE YEAR. They said it would only take an hour. They also told me chemo would only take three hours.

The good news is that my hair would start growing back now. Whatever drugs they were keeping me on do not prohibit hair growth. I would probably need to keep wearing the scarf until my hair was of acceptable style and length, but the thought of it growing back was exciting. All I could think was that by fall of 2018, I wouldn't have to worry about whether or not what lies on my head matched my outfit.

Chapter 35
The Second MRI Is Better than the First MRI

September 25th was the day that I had my second MRI to determine if the chemo had worked. The experience was far less traumatic than it was back in May. This time, I was no longer trying to wrap my head around the fact that I had cancer. This time, I wasn't trying to reconcile my hair falling out. This time I wasn't envisioning an interrupted life. This time, I was just trying to find a place of Zen while listening to Phil Collins on the headphones sing about witnessing a murder.

One of the questions they ask you before going into the tube is if you are claustrophobic. What they don't ask you is if you might be bothered by the sound as loud as a train screaming in your ears intermittently for 15 minutes. I would have answered yes to that question. Just as I was settling in and relaxing, all of a sudden, a freaking freight train noise goes off. And then they tell you not to move. Well, this goes against human nature. If something startles you out of a meditative state, you might jump a little. After they tell you not to move, they tell you not to breathe. Yes, that's right. Something loud and obnoxious is blowing out your eardrums and you are to remain still and hold your breath. It's super easy. So there went my Zen-like state.

In any case, it was all over in about 15 minutes. As I looked back, I couldn't help but think that I had come a long way. I had gone through six rounds of chemo. I had lost my hair. I had been sick for half of the four months I had been on chemo. I had returned to work. I had lived life in the best way that I could, given the circumstances. I get bitter. I get sad. I get angry. I cry. I have good days and I have bad days. I still have more ahead of me than I have behind me. But I had some pretty heavy shit behind me. I had survived this far. I would survive what came next.

This MRI marked the end of one chapter and the beginning of another. It was not over. Far from it. I would stumble along as I navigate the road ahead. I'd probably fall sometimes too. But that's what we do right? As humans? We stumble and we fall. We soar and we crash. We laugh and we cry. This is a chapter of my book, it is not my book. I will create the words. I will create the experience. Life will tell me the titles, but I will write the content.

Radiation

Chapter 36

The Radiation Oncologist

On September 30th, I went to see the radiation oncologist to talk about what happens after surgery. I was teetering between a mastectomy and lumpectomy and was leaning toward the procedure that would give me the least odds of having to do radiation. So I was really looking forward to this visit to provide some information.

The senior resident is the one who gave us all the information. A mastectomy, as you can imagine, is a massive surgery. First, you have the surgery to remove the breast (which requires a hospital stay), then you have to have another surgery to reconstruct, plus probably many doctors' visits in between. The recovery is harder and longer. With a lumpectomy, it is outpatient and pretty simple, and the recovery is understandably not as long. What I also learned was that if there is any divot in the breast after the lumpectomy, they can take the fat from other areas of the body. Basically free lips. This a nice consolation prize. So I told the resident that all of this information is great, but my fear was with radiation. I didn't want it.

Talking to a radiation oncologist about why you shouldn't have radiation is like talking to a Pepsi supplier about why you should drink Coke. They are not going to try to talk you out of it. They have made a living out of buying what it's selling. However, he was my only source of information at that time, so I was going to hear what he had to say.

I was told that radiation does not have many side effects. I may have what looks and feels like a sunburn on the treated area, and I might experience some fatigue, but nothing debilitating. He assured me that most people who have a hard time with radiation are older and bigger than I was. Since I was still young and in good health, and I exercise every day, my reactions should be minimal and manageable. I had spoken to a few people between my last surgery appointment and that one, and they had experienced this claim, so perhaps he was telling me the truth. My surgeon also said that she thinks that the fatigue from radiation might be a carry-over effect from the chemo more so than radiation itself. I can see this too. After all, I had six rounds of poison injected. It stands to reason that there might be some remnants lying around for a while.

So then I had all the information I needed. The resident went to get the doctor to put a pretty little bow on that appointment. Wow, she was a spitfire. She flew into the room and said, "I don't usually work on this side of the office, it has me turned around. Hi, my name is…" Then she started barking orders at the resident with no please or thank you, and all I was thinking was, "She must be a bitch to work under." As we got to talking, I realized that she was okay, just really abrasive. We spoke a little about my line of work and about how she had two kids in high school. She seemed like a well-versed oncologist, and I suppose that was what was most important to me right then. In time, I actually really got to like her. She is funny, smart, and oddly calming.

I decided to do a lumpectomy. The decision brought more relief than I expected. I felt like chemo might be the worst part of this. While surgery and radiation would interfere with my life, they wouldn't *change* my life like chemo has. Chemo had been killer, and I'm not even sure I realized how much until I finished it.

Chapter 37
Hair Envy

After months without hair, I started to develop some pretty serious hair envy. I was kind of hoping that I would have gotten used to the no-hair look. I mean, it was pretty easy; takes at least 10 minutes off of my get-ready time in the morning. As it turned out, I prefer hair. And I wanted it back, like, yesterday.

Some hair can stay away, like my leg and arm hair. And I wouldn't mind it if I never had to wax my upper lip again. But I needed my eyebrows to come back fully. They had gotten pretty thin, along with my lashes. Thank God for brow pencils and mascara. It's weird not to have nose hair. Who would have thought that you would lose nose hair? Well, you do, and it's weird. But the hair that I missed the most was on the top of my head.

I was noticing everyone who had beautiful, thick hair and found myself anxious to get mine back. I noticed when they did cool things with it, like brush it. I hadn't needed a brush in so long. I also noticed braids and wondered how long it would take for my hair to be long enough to braid. People's faces generally look better with hair. I hadn't looked like a complete monster with no hair, but I don't think anyone would say that I looked *better* without it.

I think the reason I had hair envy so badly was that I felt done with the chemo that caused me to lose it. When I was in the middle of chemo, there was no hope of hair, so I didn't really think about it growing back. Now it was supposed to start growing back, and it made me want it more. Realistically, I knew it wouldn't even begin growing back for at least four weeks, but that didn't stop me from checking it every day to see if I had any kind of peach fuzz on the top of my head.

*

I didn't know when it would be long enough for it to be presentable. Probably months. It wasn't like I could get rid of the scarf the minute follicles started emerging from my scalp. But when I did start to see growth, it not only meant in a matter of time I would not be a walking billboard for cancer, but more importantly, it would mean that my first part of this journey had come to an end. And this is an ending that would be marked with an exclamation point.

Chapter 38

If You're Going through Hell, Keep Going

At one point, I had two appointments in one day; one with the general surgeon and one with the plastic surgeon the other day. I think I had mentioned at some point that I had to go to several different medical facilities for my various appointments. In the last two weeks, I had to keep track of not only the different type of doctor I was seeing and the time of all the appointments, but also the location. Each doctor's visit took me to a different hospital.

My first stop was the general surgeon at 11:30. I showed up at exactly the time of the appointment. Screw the whole "be there 30 minutes early." Why should I be there 30 minutes early when you get me in 30 minutes late? Anyway, so we get there right on time, and the door is locked. We call the number and find out that they moved offices. Apparently, they said they called everyone to let them know. In the recesses of my chemo fog, I vaguely recall such a phone call, but I forgot to write it down (because I have a chemo brain and forget things far more easily). We were directed to go to the new location, which was 10 minutes away. We were 15 minutes late for our appointment, and I was breaking out in cold sweats because being late to anything causes great anxiety for me.

We finally got there and waited for about 20 minutes (not bad) before we got to see the doctor. She was the first doctor I had ever been to that I felt 100% free to talk to about any of my concerns without fear of 'doctor speak' as a response. If it weren't for the fact that she was going to be cutting into my boob, I would totally want to go have a drink with her. It's not that I love going to see any doctor, but if I must see a doctor, I am glad she is one of them.

We talked about poop. Yep. That was our conversation. Why? Because poop has been the bane of my existence. It had been in the center of my planning. My life revolved around when and if I was going to have to poop. When I would go places, I immediately looked for where the bathroom was. Poop was the reason I became more adamant about needing (not wanting) a staff only single bathroom at work. If you are a chemo survivor, you totally get it.

The reason our conversation revolved around excrement was because I explained why I did not want to use Perjeta, aka: the poop drug. I refused to live my life around poop for the next 365 days. I was just now able to drink limited amounts of coffee again, which is a diuretic in itself. Drinking it when on Perjeta yields a very unfavorable outcome. I think we talked about my feelings around this for at least half of the appointment. I feel passionately about many topics. Apparently, bowel control is one of them.

For the second half of the appointment, we talked about the actual surgery. She told me that I would need to have a two-week recovery period and to pick a date between then and November 4th. So, I chose November 7th. I explained that October is a high college application season and that I was presenting at a conference on November 5th and 6th. If she wanted me to have the surgery in October, it was unlikely that I would take the full two weeks off. So, she agreed to November 7th, and I agreed to take a full two weeks off from work.

As the appointment wrapped up, I casually asked her why I needed to see the plastic surgeon later in the day. She said since I chose a lumpectomy over a mastectomy I could cancel that appointment. So glad I asked. I would have gone to that appointment, had an extended stay in the waiting room, then I would have had an additional wait in the exam room, all to be told that I didn't need to be there at all. Casual questioning saves time.

I was just beginning to wrap my head around the fact that I was done with traditional chemo. Every time I thought about it, I felt relieved. This shit (pun intended) sucked. Like, every swear word you can imagine kind of sucked. I knew my treatment was far from over. I still had a long road ahead. But I'll keep moving because that's the only reasonable option. Like Winston Churchill said, "*If you're going through hell, keep going.*"

Chapter 39

I Feel Like It's Still a Duck

October 8, 2017, marked a week past my first chemo light treatment, which I was told is not really chemo at all. I'm not sure what makes chemo, chemo. Is there one particular drug that makes you move from liquid healing to the IV of despair? Is it like that fine line between whether you pass or fail a class; where if you get a 60% you are a winner and get to collect your credits to go on to the next round, but if you get a 59% then you are deemed a failure who needs remedial help?

I had four drugs: Carboplatin, Taxotere, Perjeta, and Herceptin. The only one that I was keeping was Herceptin. I was told that this is not chemo, but I went to the same place where I had been going for treatments. I was asked the same questions, spoke to the same doctor, saw the same people, and sat in the same chair. I mean, if it looks like a duck and talks like a duck, then.... So whatever fancy name the doctor wanted to call it, it's chemo light to me.

The last heavy chemo treatment was miserable. Side effects lasted almost right up until the time of the first chemo light treatment. Mostly the side effects that come with Perjeta, which, if you have been following, is lots of poop.

I sat in the chemo chair to get my not chemo treatment. It lasted for 35 minutes. I mean, the whole appointment lasted for about two hours because of all the waiting. The waiting really is the hardest part, Tom Petty, it really is. But going from four and a half hours of IV drips to 35 minutes is extremely liberating. It's like when you come home from work and take off your constricting business attire and change into your PJs because it's 5:00 and daylight savings time has ended so it's dark, which means it's nighttime, which means PJs are totally appropriate.

I was officially four weeks post regular chemo. The thing about pounding poisons into your body for four months is that it tends to take longer to get out of your system. I was still experiencing some side effects, although none that were debilitating. Every now and again my fingers felt numb, and my eyesight seemed to be getting worse. Joint pain appeared to be a problem, to the point where I had woken up in the middle of the night in tears because I couldn't straighten my leg. I was told to go to an orthopedic doctor for some sort of steroid shot.

All things considering, physically I felt the best I had ever felt since this whole thing began. This is probably largely due to the fact that I didn't ever have to do another chemotherapy treatment again. That shit is no joke. I'm not sure I fully realized how horrible it was until I looked back and wondered how I did it.

Chapter 40

Look Me in the Eye
(and other reflections on chemo)

You know how sometimes you don't understand the magnitude of something until it is over? Like, when there is a tornado warning and the sky turns green and wind gains speed. You think to yourself, "Well, this doesn't look good," so you grab all your valuables and set up camp in the basement. When it's over, you come out from hiding to assess the damage. It is then you realize the roof of your house was blown off, your windows shattered, and your favorite stuffed animal you had as a child is gone. That's kind of what the end of chemo felt like to me.

I remember the warning—the doctor telling me how many rounds of chemo I needed, that my hair was going to fall out, and how my summer would pretty much suck, but that there would be more great summers ahead. I remember my reaction, mainly tears and fear.

As the first round of six approached, I set up camp in my personal basement, waiting for the storm to pass. I lost my hair there. I got sick there. I played 'normal' there so as not to let anyone know that this was getting the better of me. The chemo storm passed around October 18th, at least that's when I started resembling myself again. At that point, I straightened out my scarf, stood up tall, and walked outside to assess the damage.

The thing about storms is that you can't really tell what the worst part is. Is it the anticipation leading up to it, when it is happening, or when it is over? Maybe they are all equally bad in different ways. I go into survival mode when faced with any crisis. This allows me to not feel my emotions as deeply as I should at the time of the event because I need all my faculties to get through it. Then when it is over, I look back and think, "Holy hell, did I just do that?"

Some people have been through far worse than I have, but if you know me, I don't play the whole *somebody has it worse* game. That's a stupid game designed to invalidate someone else's experience. For me, this is the worst thing that I have been through. It was, and is, like emotional boot camp. My hair falling out symbolized the tearing you down part that they talk about in boot camp. I was still waiting to get built back up.

October 24th marked five months since my initial diagnosis and one month past my last chemo treatment. I found myself getting overwhelmed with emotion. I mean, what the hell did I just do? The fatigue, the stomach issues, the horrible taste in my mouth all the time, among other things. But it was over (the chemo anyway), and I was supposed to be fine. But I was not totally fine. It's like that feeling after someone dies and the funeral is over. The condolences have all been said, the flowers and food have been delivered, and you are left sitting by yourself wondering what you are supposed to do next. How are you supposed to feel now?

All I know for certain is that when a storm passes, whether physical or emotional, it doesn't leave you the same. This isn't unique to cancer. This is true of any tragedy. What I also know is that if you don't look into the eye of the storm, you will never know how bad it is. And if you can't assess the damage, you can't fully recover.

I often found myself in a staring contest.

Chapter 41
The Parking Lot

In business, there is a name that is given when you have an idea or thought that you would like to discuss later. It is called the parking lot. The purpose of the parking lot is to not interrupt the flow of the meeting with your silly thoughts but instead, allow for a place for you to put your comments. In my experience, this place has been a table in the corner that will eventually be filled with sticky notes of wonderings. During question and answer time, the facilitator will grab some of these sticky notes and address the thoughts, ideas, or concerns.

I had been using this parking lot when it comes to cancer. Turns out, it was causing quite a traffic jam. I was scheduled for surgery in a week. I was a little bit of a mess. I was so overwhelmed with the things that I had to get done at work before my leave. Or maybe I was creating the illusion of being overwhelmed so I didn't have to think of what was to come. Probably a little of both.

When you're going through something you just kind of do it. I have found this to be especially true for women. No offense men, but we women are rock stars. We juggle so many things that you don't even know about because we don't talk about them. And when tragedy strikes, we are usually the ones that keep the ship sailing. We are the life preservers for our family. This time, I had put the life preserver on myself so I could keep my own ship moving. I sailed through the roughest waters (chemo) and felt like I could breathe a little, so I took off my life preserver. Stupid. I was having a hard time breathing now.

It wouldn't make any sense to someone who hasn't gone through something big. But for those who have, this makes total sense. It doesn't have to be cancer. It could be a death, a divorce, or some other life-altering event. The fact is, when it is finally okay to breathe, we find ourselves suffocating.

I mentioned earlier in this book that one of my biggest fears is being found out, essentially being found out that I have no idea what I am doing and am really quite stupid. So after some self-reflection, it hit me that part of my anxiety stemmed from having two weeks off work. Someone else would have to pick up the slack. My slack. And in doing so, they might find that I was stupid. What if I forgot to dot an 'I' or cross a 't'? What if whoever covered for me was so much better than me that all my colleagues and students would be really bummed upon my return? What if all the insecurities I kept hidden became reality? What if? What if? What if?

When my anxiety becomes too much, it is usually because I am contending with some unresolved issues. Right then, my anxiety was equivalent to that of the entire continent of Asia. This told me I needed to stop and assess the situation. But when I looked around, all I saw was a really full parking lot. I left all of my fears at the table in the corner so I could carry on with the task at hand and not be interrupted by silly little self-talk. Now the meeting is paused, and I need to take a look at all my sticky notes of wonderings.

- I wonder if I will come out of this okay.
- I wonder if this will change me for the worse.
- I wonder if all the medication will make me gain weight.
- I wonder if people won't think I am pretty anymore.
- I wonder if the cancer will return.

Typically, in a parking lot when we are crammed between two cars that didn't leave enough room for us to open our door to get in, it is valuable to assess the situation before blindly opening the driver's side door and smashing it against the car next to you. This case is no different. At some point, I was going to have to stop and breathe, walk over to the parking lot, and start moving cars. It was the only way I would ever get out.

Ultimately, I decided to take a breath and slowly get out of the chemo car so I could slowly walk over to my next ride. Surgery.

Chapter 42

Surgery

On November 7th, I was scheduled to have a lumpectomy. This involved a simple procedure of cutting into my right breast and removing the cancerous 'lump'.

It's funny how to a surgeon, this type of operation is simple. But to me, the patient, it wasn't so easy. The procedure might involve a simple cut of the skin and small incision, but to me, it involved so much more.

This was my breast. This was part of what made me a woman. Even though I never really cared so much about them, the thought of having anything done to them threatened my identity once more. So I was nervous. Not as nervous as I was the day I started chemotherapy, but angry nervous that the road didn't seem like it was ever going to end. It set me on a path that I fear I will never find my way back from.

I was scheduled for surgery on November 7, 2017. Like most surgeries, I was required me to be at the hospital early, at 6 AM. We spent the night at Joe's mom's house because she was watching Jacob while we were gone.

I am already an anxious person. But when I have somewhere important to be, or perhaps required to get my body cut open, I get a little extra anxious. I survey all the things around me that I can control. The list seemed to be getting thinner by the minute, which only meant that my anxiety was getting bigger by the minute.

I set the alarm at an appropriate time, which for me was about 40 minutes before I actually needed to get up. You know, in case something happened that I didn't account for. I got in the shower, then told Joe to get in the shower. I sat anxiously while I waited for him to be ready.

Joe is not anxious. Like, at all. His modus operandi is "It'll all work out." When I counter with a "Yes, but," he always says, "When hasn't it worked out?" This is annoying but accurate.

The morning of the surgery, I needed Joe to be a little more anxious. I tried to keep my crazy locked in, recognizing that my thoughts were irrational, but when Joe went to make a cup of tea at the exact time I thought we should be leaving, I almost started to cry. This was not the plan.

Now I know he was right when he said that they never get us in on time anyway, and I also knew he was right when he said that making tea was not going to ruin our time frame. So let me preface this by saying I don't really blame Joe for making a cup of tea. BUT did I mention that I have anxiety? When one has anxiety, it is important to control the things you can. I could not control cancer, doctor's appointments, surgeries, side effects, lost hair. But I *could* control the time we left. Making a cup of tea was not in my morning plans. But I am finding when other humans are involved, the amount of control diminishes by the number of humans.

The situation was magnified a bit when Jacob woke up and clung to me for dear life. The poor guy was scared, and there was really nothing I could do to make him not scared. So imagine yourself already on level 10 when your nine-year-old is crying and clinging to you. This has a way of bringing you back down to level 4. Looking at Jacob and seeing how worried he was for me allowed me to put things in perspective. Arriving late to the hospital wouldn't result in my surgery getting canceled. But arriving late to the hospital might mean that I had a few extra minutes to soothe the anxiety of my worried child.

I decided to remember what was important and take the time to help my son feel comfortable. Soon my mother-in-law came down the stairs, took Jacob to go watch some TV, and all was well.

We got into the car at 5:35, five minutes later than I wanted. Not too bad. Joe plugged in the route on the navigation system and said that our ETA was 6:02. Perfect.

So perfection is a funny thing. It implies that there is no error. Now we all know that there is always some error, so really there is no such thing as pure perfection. We got halfway into our drive and Joe says "SHIT." Okay, so let me just take this time to offer a public service announcement. When dealing with someone with anxiety, yelling 'Oh shit' is not the best way for said person to feel at ease. Naturally, I asked what was wrong. Turns out we were going to Royal Oak Beaumont. We were supposed to be going to Troy Beaumont. This adds about 15 more minutes to our trip. Our ETA was now 6:17, 17 minutes past the time we were supposed to be there. Now is a good time for me to practice my breathing exercises. I don't have breathing exercises. Now is a good time to create some breathing exercises.

Joe, in his never-ending attempt to help me not to worry, started driving about 90 mph down the highway. In my head, I scripted what I would say if we got pulled over. Because when you have anxiety, you go through all of the possible scenarios—getting pulled over, getting into an accident and if your anxiety is severe enough, even death. I would tell the officer that I have cancer and was late for surgery. Then in my head, the officer would escort us to the hospital. We did not get pulled over, but Joe shaved four minutes off of our drive time.

So we got to the hospital. I had my book ready because the wait time is always at least 45 minutes. It's cute that I thought I would be calm enough to read. Naturally, I was not.

The receptionist called both Joe and me to the desk. She told me that I would see the radiologist first, then go have a mammogram (these two things I did not know. I thought I was going straight to surgery), then we would go get prepped for surgery. She told Joe he could help himself to anything on the refreshment table. I responded that I was a little disappointed in the hospitality shown to the patients, as we were not allowed to eat or drink anything, yet you lay a table of coffee and snacks right in front of us. This was said humorously, of course. When I get nervous, I get extra sarcastic. Some who know me may think it impossible for me to be more sarcastic, but I assure you, it happens.

I didn't even get a chance to sit down before the nurse took me back. Really? NOW is the time that you are going to be efficient? I had my book. I was ready to wait, and now you decide not to waste my time. I finally figured out the game and you changed the rules!

I went back to the holding cell, where a very efficient nurse was doing a multitude of things. I imagined that she might be a supervisor because the other nurse kept asking her questions. I also imagined that she might have a wig on because her hair looked synthetic. I did not ask this question because what if that was her real hair? This woman was putting needles in me. I didn't want to tick her off.

The radiologist who entered the room seemed bored. His words were lackluster, and he moved slowly. He generally seemed a little annoyed to be there. I get it, buddy. I'm a little annoyed too. In any case, he stuck a needle in me. I don't know what was in that needle. They told me, but true to how I had been handling this whole cancer thing, I didn't really pay attention. I figured a radiologist comes in and wants to poke a needle in you, it must be for good reason.

After a while, I got wheeled to the mammography room where they take some Glamour Shots of my right breast. Then they shot me with some numbing stuff. At least that's what I think they said. Again, I wasn't really paying attention. What I paid attention to was the fact that I was about to faint. I got nauseous and the color dissipated from my face. They had to lay me down so I would return to a normal state. The nurse talked to me about how this was not an uncommon reaction to stress. I knew this already, but it was good to be reminded. Even when you can convince your mind that everything is going to be okay, it is much harder to convince your body. This explains the random crying fits I had over the last week.

Finally, I was wheeled back to the surgery holding cell and they brought Joe and the surgeon back. Have I

149

mentioned that I love my surgeon? She is my kind of people. Funny, sarcastic, down to earth. We talked about how her day was filled with thinking about all the different iPhone apps she could invent. This is not a typical conversation before going into surgery, but I loved it. It took my mind off what was about to happen. Perhaps that was her plan.

She told me and Joe the more important things about the surgery (how long it would take, what to expect after, etc.). Then she and Joe left and someone came in to administer the anesthesia. This was the part I had been waiting for. I love anesthesia. There is nothing that I have experienced that can mirror this kind of restful sleep. Also, it makes a one and a half hour surgery feel like 30 seconds.

I remember the needle, and then I remember waking up.

When surgery was over, I woke up to a very tight-fitting bra that was supposed to help minimize pain with movement. All I could think was "When did they put this on me?" In any case, aside from the hour that Joe had to wait for me to wake up, there was no wait time after surgery. I got up, got dressed, and we were in the car by 1 PM. When I got home, I ate a very large bowl of chili and went back to sleep.

That experience wasn't so bad. I had some pain from where the incision was, and I imagined I would be in an anesthetic fog for a few days, but chemo still ranks as the biggest bitch of cancer. I can deal with some physical pain. It is much more bearable than the internal pain that chemo brings. I would know in my follow up appointment if they got all the cancer out. But given that the chemo shrank it so much already, I was left feeling optimistic about the results. Optimism felt good. I hadn't felt it for a while.

So that was my surgery day. A few comedic errors, a sad child, an almost fainting spell, a bored doctor, a nurse who may or may not be wearing a wig, a surgeon who could be a comedian; surgery was a breeze.

Chapter 43

Tamoxifen

Recovering from surgery was not too bad for me. But these damn pills made me feel like I was losing my mind. After surgery, my oncologist started me on Tamoxifen. This is a pill for patients with hormone-receptor-positive, early-stage breast cancer, typically taken after surgery and chemotherapy to reduce the risk of the cancer coming back. Side effects include moodiness, fatigue, depression, headaches, and hot flashes. I usually don't pay attention to side-effects because I never have any. This time, I had them all.

These damn pills made me feel like I was losing my mind. The hot flashes were so intense that I had sweat beading down my face and back multiple times a day. It was worse at night. The fatigue was constant. I thought I was done feeling tired after chemo, but apparently, this is a gift that keeps on giving. No amount of sleep helped me feel refreshed. I felt lackluster about life in general. This was probably the worst feeling. My anxiety levels were higher than normal, and I found myself getting angry more easily. It's not that I'm not generally happy. It's more like the feeling of walking in a strange land with a full bladder. All you want to do is find the bathroom, but no one understands the language you are speaking, so you find yourself screaming into a crowd full of people who are just staring at you and wondering what the problem is.

At one point, the side-effects of Tamoxifen were so bad that Joe sent friends to check up on me. He thought I might do something stupid. Probably because I told him that I felt both homicidal and suicidal. To this day, I have never experienced such horrible emotions all at once. The agitation and anger were almost insurmountable.

I was given a 90-day supply of this horrible drug, plus three refills. That's 270 days. I couldn't feel that way for 270 days. My husband and son should not have to live with someone who felt that way for 270 days. I could manage it enough to fool the outside world. If anyone asked me, I would say I was doing fine. I had enough mental clarity to understand that this was a temporary situation requiring intentional coping strategies. I was putting these strategies into place. I knew they would help me feel balanced and in control until I could get to a better place. So I created a schedule.

I had two weeks off work to recover from surgery. I tried to relax, but the Tamoxifen was making me crazy. I don't have an easy time relaxing in general. I have an easy time being lazy, but being lazy and relaxing are two different things. I can't get my mind to shut off. I had a book, I had found a show on Netflix that I could binge on, I had time to figure out how to create a survey on Google Docs. It takes effort to do any of these things.

I had taken to making lists so I could force myself to participate in my existence. My list included exercising, going to the dry cleaner, going to the store to get paper towels, cleaning the bathrooms, cleaning my closet, and walking the dog. Through my rage, fatigue, and general bad attitude, I still managed to do everything on the list. It felt good to be productive. And the cold November air helped me to recenter my mind.

Chapter 44

#Cancerfree

It was November 13, 2017. This day is important because it was the day the doctor called me to tell me I was officially cancer-free. She likened my cancer to Swiss cheese. The analogy was that before chemo, the cancer was like cheddar cheese. Solid and visible. After surgery, it was like Swiss cheese. Swiss cheese cancer means that there is less than 5% of viable cancer cells, which means it is insignificant, which meant I was considered CANCER FREE!

The funny part is that she started the conversation by telling me "First, the lymph nodes are good. No cancer detected." Then there was a pregnant pause. It was then that I realized I was a little nervous. Was she about to tell me they didn't get it all? Or worse, they found more? When someone pauses before they share news with you, your mind has a funny way of bringing to the surface all the fears that lay dormant. The elation that my body felt when I heard the words 'cancer-free' told me that the anxiety that it had been feeling was partly due to my concern that I may never be cancer-free. The other part is totally the Tamoxifen.

So cancer is like cheese.

I like cheese.

Cheese is good.

Chapter 45
The Radiation Simulator

I had the luxury of living the last month or so in a fog of denial. Aside from the chemo light, which is really more of a nuisance than anything, I hadn't really had to think about cancer. On December 18ᵗʰ, I was pushed back into reality as I went for my radiation simulation appointment.

I was told that I needed to have six weeks of radiation. Unlike chemo or chemo light, this would happen every day. Also, unlike chemo or chemo light, I got to choose when it happened. I chose 3:15 PM, Monday to Friday. I got weekends off because apparently cancer doesn't live on the weekends. Before beginning the actual radiation, they needed to do a simulation to prep my body for the beam of light that would kill what was left of my cancer.

They gave me a key ring with a bar code label on it. I was told that I was to present this every day. If I didn't, they would have to ask me my name and birthday each time I come. Can you imagine the major inconvenience of asking anyone what their name and birth date is? So instead of helping radiation patients feel like humans by actually conversing with us, we had been reduced to a bar code.

When they took me up to the simulation room, I was greeted by another radiation therapist and the intern. Both men were younger than me and attractive. That felt weird to me. I couldn't help but to think about what they were like when they were at a bar. Were they sleazy? Were they respectful? Did they talk about how many boobs they saw that day? They were both very professional, but it is still awkward to be voluntarily exposing my breast to two strange men.

After they adjusted and contorted my body to fit onto what looked like an MRI machine, they placed wires on both breasts. I don't really know why. I figured it makes them do their job better. Then, and here's the best part, they got out a little camera and took a picture of my breast. My naked, exposed breast. I immediately felt a little dirty. They did it to measure progress I'm sure, but it still felt a little bit like soft porn.

Then they told me all the side effects that I may or may not have. Burning on the area being radiated, fatigue, one breast might swell a bit. This is fantastic. What's even more fantastic is I was told that it shouldn't be too bad. How the hell did they know? I hate it when people who have never been through something tell me how it will be. In any case, it's happening whether I like it or not. I was scheduled to start actual radiation on January 2nd. It sucked, but it also signified that I was getting to where I wanted to be.

Chapter 46
Journey to the Center of My Bald Spot

In late December, I noticed that my hair was starting to grow back. It was coming in baby fine. I was not sure if the color was brown or dark gray, but I knew that I had one patch right in the front that was coming in white. So that's beautiful. I legitimately looked like Sinead O'Connor. If I were a braver woman, I would've taken off my scarf and just owned it. But not only was I not that brave, but it was – 4 degrees in Michigan, and I was cold. Turns out being bald *does* cause it to feel like it is 10 degrees colder. So, in my reality, it was – 14 degrees without my headscarf. The scarf stayed on.

The hair on my legs, arms, and face was also coming back. This was not welcomed. Because the hair was so light and fine, I didn't even notice that it was coming back until I happened to look at myself in a magnified mirror and saw long black hair coming out of my chin. Damn it. I was kind of hoping that would be something that wouldn't return. The lack of hair on my face caused it to clear up because there was nothing to clog the pores. Having cancer, early menopause, and prepubescent acne, left me to determine that there is no justice for suffering.

I shaved my legs for the first time in seven months. Apparently, I forgot how to use a razor because I gave myself a pretty deep cut on my leg. Screw it. It was winter. I had at least another three months before I showed my legs again. I'm putting down the razor. Sorry, Joe. But to be fair, you couldn't see or really feel it. That's how soft it was.

I'd gotten pretty used to my look in a scarf. I was thinking about keeping it for bad hair days. I figured at the rate my hair was growing, it would be next Fall before I was comfortable walking around without my head covered. In any case, it was good to see pieces of life come back to my body. The small hairs, no matter how fine or how slowly they grew or how gray they might have been, reminded me that my journey was nearing an end. The scar on my right breast and the scar that would be left when they took out my port a year later would serve as a reminder of the journey that I had taken.

I really appreciated the radiologist allowing me to get through the holidays before starting radiation. Suddenly, for the first time in eight months, I would be free of any doctor's visits for a good three weeks. For a minute, I would feel normal, like someone who didn't have cancer. I longed for that feeling.

Christmas 2016 was filled with the same spirit of joy and happiness that it had been in every previous year. My constant diarrhea had subsided and while I was tired, I had enough energy to get through the entire season feeling happy and pretending to be healthy.

In January, I began radiation therapy. I chose 3:15 PM as my daily radiation time. This way I could leave work just 20 minutes early, go to radiation, and be home in time to pick up Jacob from school.

They told me that radiation would only take 10 minutes. "As soon as you get here, you are leaving," they said. I knew that could not possibly be true. There is no doctor on the planet that I had experienced who does not make you wait an annoying amount of time past your scheduled appointment to be seen.

However, while I wasn't in and out in a flash, they really did do a great job of adhering to my 3 PM appointment.

My first day of radiation was a bit awkward. There were two radiation techs. One was a man and one was a woman. They were a bit younger than me but were so personable that they immediately made me feel comfortable. What was even better was that they got my sense of humor, which not everyone does. I have a very dry, sarcastic humor that can be off-putting to people who do not understand it.

As soon as I got on the table to be radiated, Matt, the male technician started talking about his wife and kids. I am sure this was a calculated move to make me feel comfortable that he was about to see me exposed and have his hands all over my breasts.

It worked. I felt at ease over the course of the weeks of radiation, and I developed a nice relationship with both Matt and Nicole. I learned that Nicole was an only child who was hoping to be engaged by March 2017. Matt was married with three young children. I also learned that he really appreciates nice scents, and he always told me how good I smelled (not in a creepy way).

It's funny how going through something so horrible helps you connect to people. I guess when you are around the same people so often, you are bound to have some kind of a relationship.

I had gotten into a rhythm with radiation, and the Radiologists had gotten into a rhythm with me. If there were any issues with time that occurred the first week, they had subsided and I was in and out of there within 30 minutes. Except Wednesdays. Wednesdays, I had to see the doctor. I guessed to make sure that I am not glowing, but more likely to make sure the burns on my skin were not too bad. So far they had not been. I was supposed to be using some sort of cream. I was not using it. I don't know why I was resistant to walking to the pharmacy next door to the doctor's office to collect the cream. The nurse ordered it for me. All I had to do was pick it up. But I had no desire. I don't know, maybe it was because I was so tired of all the prescriptions. Maybe I'm just lazy. I am sure that there is some sort of profound psychological reason why I was not walking the 10 steps from the doctor's office to the pharmacy.

I also found that I kept forgetting the tag that was supposed to scan into the computer so I didn't have to keep telling them my birthday before I got radiated. I think I know the psychology behind not wearing it. It is a tag. It is a number to be scanned. I am a number to be scanned.

I am not a number to be scanned, so I didn't wear it. I didn't do this consciously, but I am sure I was subconsciously purposely forgetting to put it on because I didn't want anyone to lose sight of the fact that I am a human being.

There was an older gentleman and his wife whom I would see every day. When you have an assigned time to get treatment, you tend to see the same people every day. Much like chemotherapy, radiation is the extension of the club. Anyway, this man was getting treated for prostate cancer and it was his 2nd round apparently. I really liked this couple. They were funny and made me laugh as I sat awkwardly in my hospital gown waiting to be called back. Two days previous, he finished his last round of his 2nd round. He got to ring a bell, say goodbye to everyone, and leave. I wouldn't be seeing him again, but I sure did appreciate the two weeks I had to get to know him.

I was scheduled to have my last treatment on February 13th. So far, I felt no side effects except for a little fatigue. But who could tell if being tired was from the treatment, because it was winter and cold, or from working and having a child?

As the weeks of radiation continued, I found it much more doable than I originally thought. Besides the annoyance of having to try to wrap everything up at work by 2:30 so that I could be at my appointment on time every day, it wasn't too bad. I realized that I may have been one of the lucky ones, not everyone gets off so easily. I had redness where the radiation was being targeted, but it didn't feel like a sunburn as I was told it would. It really didn't give me any irritation at all. I used no cream aside from the typical body cream I use daily. I noticed my face was itchy. I don't know if this was because it was exposed to the radiation or just because it was winter and the air was dry. But it was annoying nonetheless.

Chapter 46b

What I Learned from Radiation

I have learned of three things to make sure you do when undergoing radiation.

1. Keep 'em guessing with your scarf choices (I always wore a different scarf).
2. Wear a pretty scented lotion.
3. Pay attention to your shoes.

Most of the time I was coming from work, which meant I was dressed in work attire. Just because I had lost my hair didn't mean I had lost my love of a good ensemble. The scarf on the top of my head served as an accessory. I had scarves in all different colors. They matched my mood and my outfit. I tied them like I would a messy bun, using a rubber band. When I really want to class it up, I add a flower pin or bedazzled barrette on the side.

The radiation therapists had branded me as the 'girl who smells nice'. This made me feel good. One, it is nice to know that the lotion I wore still had a scent after eight hours of wear, and two, it is nice to have that kind of label. I'll take it.

Shoes are probably the most important accessory you will wear while undergoing radiation treatment. Reason being, you are lying flat on a table, and if the radiologists don't want to stare at your exposed breasts, they naturally need to look somewhere. This is usually your feet. Thankfully, I love a good shoe.

It feels good to walk into a cancer treatment facility and be noticed for everything other than my cancer. This is probably because, just like the 4.0 GPA student who applies to U of M, I am a dime a dozen in this place. What set me apart was my scarf, my scent, and my shoes. It was nice to walk out of a place knowing that the people in it will describe me as the girl with the classy scarves, pretty scent, and nice shoes, instead of the girl who has cancer.

Where my patience wore thin was the wait time at chemo light. I would take 10 more weeks of radiation to not have to wait more than 30 minutes at a doctor's office. My last appointment at the oncologist was scheduled for 9:45. If I had bet $5 that I wouldn't get out of there until 12:30 at the earliest, I would have been $5 richer.

To put this into perspective, my treatment was only 20 minutes. I should have only had to take a half-day off work to get treatment, but because of the level of wait time, I had to take a full day off of work.

This journey has left me with a disdain for the medical world. Not the actual treatment part, my doctors seem to be good at that, but the general loss of memory on the doctor's part that their patient is also a human, who has a life, has places to be, and cannot wait for hours for you to see them. I'm also not okay with the level of greeting I was still getting from the receptionists at chemo light. Upon check-in, they did not make eye contact and seemed annoyed that I was there (believe me, I am more annoyed). They didn't even acknowledge my existence. Last time, the receptionist actually looked at me and then picked up the phone and called someone. REALLY? Come on. A little more compassion and acknowledgment would've been appreciated. I'm happy to wait, but please tell me you will be with me in a moment, don't make me guess.

My hair was growing back. I still couldn't tell if it was coming in gray or ash blonde. Doesn't really matter. To me, both of those shades were gross, so I planned to reconnect with L'Oréal. I was just happy to see hair on my head again. It was going to be a while before I felt comfortable without a scarf, but it was there, and it was growing.

The upside of losing all your hair, especially if you are a woman, is that as it grows back, you get to try out all those short hairstyles you always wanted to try but were too afraid to cut off your long hair. So much like my doctor's appointments, the short would feel long.

Chapter 47

Is It Over Yet?

The last day of radiation finally arrived. I celebrated by picking my son up from school because he had a low-grade fever. This was just one of life's daily reminders that the world does not revolve around me.

In any case, it was OVER. The big treatments were done. I still had Herceptin (i.e. chemo light) treatments every three weeks until the end of May, but everything that could, and did make me sick, burn my skin, make my hair fall out, give me a metal taste in my mouth, make my fingernails break, my eyesight change, my brain become stupid, cause my hearing to deteriorate, and make me want to sleep 24/7 was OVER. I was done being a slave to toxins that ran through my veins. I moved from a person who has cancer, to a person who had lived through cancer.

This was not worth it. Let me be clear. I am not thankful for any of this. I am not one of those people who have woken up and said to myself that I am thankful for having cancer because it made me the person that I am today. Nope. I am quite sure that we all have a trajectory to follow, and I would become the person I am today without the hassle.

This was a piece of my story; it is not the whole story. It is not even a fraction of the story. It is a defining moment, but it is not THE defining moment.

I don't really believe that there is one defining moment. I believe that all moments define who we are, and we are constantly changing and experiencing moments that will continue to define us. We are humans and we are meant to evolve. Cancer is one moment that helped define me, but you know what else did?

Going to college

Getting married

Infertility

Losing an adopted child

Adopting a child

Changing careers

My coworkers

Making friends

Losing friends

There is more, but you get my point. A defining moment, in my opinion, is one that can be big or small. It is anything that brings self-awareness. It might be that time that someone said something that resonated with you and helped shape the way you view things. It does not have to be something big, or something that we are thankful for. It just is.

We get the lessons we are meant to have. I believe that.

We should strive to fill our world with people and things that are diverse enough to make us challenge ourselves, step outside our comfort zones, see things from a different perspective. Cancer did these things for me, but so did many other things. There are still so many other defining moments that I have to experience. I will take the lessons from each of them and try to improve who I am. I am in a constant mission for self-improvement. We all should be.

My journey was not over. I still had months to go. But the treatment I had left was more annoying than painful. I've learned a lot from this experience, I still am. Self-education is the most useful education one can get.

Chapter 48

I Am on My Way

It was a random Thursday morning. I got out of the shower, dried myself off as I normally do, put on my robe, and went upstairs to get dressed. I glanced at my reflection in the mirror and almost cried. My hair was still wet. Normally, after I dry it off with a towel, by the time I get upstairs, it is completely dry. But on this day, it was still wet, which meant that it was thick enough to hold moisture. I had hair thick enough to remain wet for at least five minutes after washing it. I was on my way.

Another instance where I cried was at my last radiation appointment. They have you ring this bell, signifying the end of radiation treatment. I walked past the bell when Nicole, the technician, called me back and told me I have to ring it. "Fine," I said. But it felt kind of stupid, and I really didn't want the sound of the bell ringing to call attention to me in any way. But I am a people pleaser, so I rang the damn bell. I was suddenly flooded with unanticipated emotion. My eyes started to well up. I was on my way.

Crying is not something entirely unusual for me. I am a crier. But the tears that I had been shedding as I wrapped up this chapter were different than anything I have felt before.

It felt as if I had been holding my breath since May, and I finally exhaled. I was on my way.

I was done with radiation and real chemotherapy (still had chemo light, which is really just a Herceptin treatment every three weeks). I made it. There were times that I didn't think that I would. There were times that I wanted to be so enveloped in my own self-pity that I didn't want to face the reality of what was happening to me. There were times that my anger was so encompassing that I felt like I would never know what happy felt like again. There were times of uncertainty, there were times of grief. But now? Now there are times of hope. I was on my way.

I didn't know if I would get there. I mean, I knew I would get there physically, but I thought I might break along the way. I didn't feel as strong as I knew I had to be. But then again, sometimes strength is just getting out of bed. And I did get out of bed. I got out of bed every day. I don't think we should discredit the power of getting out of bed. For some of us, it is all we can do.

At some point, I knew I would take the time to reflect on the culmination of all that I had been through. But for now, I was just going to sit there and exhale. I was not ready to look back yet. All I wanted to do was be where I was. And at this moment, I was satisfied just to be on my way.

Chapter 49

Look Before You Jump

I have learned something about myself. I'm not a jump in headfirst kind of person. I like to dip a toe in to test the temperature before I submerge my entire being into the water. This is not entirely new information, but it is interesting how it plays out in my life.

Hair growing back after chemo is awkward. I mean, you know you have to lose it, so you eventually embrace the bald and find cute scarves to wear on your head and learn how to tie them in a fashionable way. Now people are used to you with a scarf. They have told you that you look good. You feel like you look okay too. Then the hair grows back, and now you have a dilemma. How long does it have to be before you choose to unwrap your head? I mean, people are now used to you in a scarf; taking it off will mean you will have to again live through the initial shock and awe at your new look.

It seemed that my way of handling this was to start showing people, one by one, what my head looked like. I found myself doing this at work, with some friends. I even posted a picture of my look on a friend's Facebook page. I think I was subconsciously trying to prepare people so that I could avoid the shock and awe. That way, when I decided to make the reveal, people would be like, "Eh, I've seen that before," and go about their day.

When I was diagnosed with cancer and realized that losing my hair was inevitable, I was so focused on being bald that I didn't stop to think about the complication of my hair growing back. You wouldn't think this would be complicated, but it really is. People were noticing the hair at the base of my neck, and it made me wonder if it would start to look really stupid if I continued to wear a scarf as it got longer.

Just like my hair was my security blanket before chemo, my scarf had become something of a security blanket after chemo. At some point, I needed to realize that security shouldn't come from what lies on the top of my head. I was not quite there yet.

Somewhere along the line, I went from being a people watcher to the person being watched. I used to be able to sit on a bench, or walk down a crowded street unnoticed, and look at the people passing. I would make up stories in my head about their lives. Sometimes, I would get lost in their story until something or someone shocked me back into reality. People watching is definitely a favorite pastime of mine.

I was in Chicago over the weekend. Chicago. A perfect place to people watch incognito. As I casually admired the made-up stories of the people passing by, I realized that the gazes were on me. Not just a quick glance, but once overs accompanied by a quizzical look. I felt exposed and uncomfortable. It had been a good nine months of scarf-wearing. By then, it had become a fixture on my head that I almost didn't notice anymore. Almost.

Chicago made me remember that it was not an invisible head covering, and that it did make me stick out in a crowd. People are curious when a white girl walks around with a headscarf on. So curious that they unapologetically stare. They stared so much that I was beginning to think I had a giant growth on my nose. But then I did something I have never done before.

I flipped the script.

I decided that I can still make up stories about people, even when they are watching me. And so the stories I made up were that these people were looking at me with admiration instead of sympathy. They were admiring the way I tied my scarf and the little flower accent that I put on it for decoration.

Flipping the script helped me to walk a little taller that weekend. The stories we tell ourselves are powerful dictators of our outlook. The way we carry ourselves is often determined by the little voices in our heads. For too long, my little voice was screaming at me that I am not good enough without my hair. But that Chicago weekend, that same voice was telling me that I am a confident woman who adorns her scarf as a way to accentuate her personality. It doesn't say ignore me. Instead, it says look at me. This is what a survivor looks like.

Chapter 50

A Series of Misfortunate Events

I had my Herceptin treatment the day after I got back from Chicago. Or at least I thought I had a treatment the day after I got back from Chicago. Why did I think I had an appointment? Because I got a text message from the doctor's office two days before reminding me of it. It just so happened that this was the ONE time that I did not put my appointment in my calendar, so I had to rely on the people in charge of my treatment. How stupid of me. Anyway, the day of my non-existent treatment turned out to be a series of misfortunate events.

First, I got into the room where they take my weight, height, and stick a needle in my port. I found an open seat and sat down. The medical assistant pointed to another seat. Words. Words would have worked here because when you use words I am more likely to understand what you are saying. But okay. I will take the pointing finger and look of "What are you, stupid?" on her face to mean that I had chosen the wrong chair. When she was done, she put me in a room where I waited for the doctor. Strike one.

First, the physician's assistant came in and told me that I was a week early, to which I reply, "Well, this office told me to come in today." Then the doctor comes in and also tells me I am a week early, to which my reply is the same, followed by digital evidence of the text message. Now you are expecting an apology, right? If you are holding your breath for one, you might die because it ain't comin'. Their response was, "We send text reminders?" They were puzzled by this for a few long seconds before I had to remind them that wasn't really the point. The point is that I had taken time off work to be there because of something that was not my fault. So, my consolation prize was that I got to take more time off work the following week, but I didn't have to see the doctor, I could just go right on back to the chemo chair. The doctor seemed to be happy with this compromise. I was not. Strike two.

Finally, I got to the receptionist's desk to check out and schedule my next appointment. It was my favorite receptionist. She liked to pick up the phone as I stood in front of her and eat a snack, all while ignoring my presence. On a good day, she avoided the phone and was just rude. Today must have been a good day.

I told her the miscommunication, to which she says, "We have you down for today." Breathe, Monica, breathe. I politely explained that the office made a mistake and the doctor wanted to see me next week. She asked me how long my appointment lasts, to which I tell her that the treatment is 20 minutes, the wait is three hours. She laughed. I guess that was funny. "Well, the only time we have is next Wednesday at 12:30." Why was she so disturbed? It wasn't her appointment that got screwed up. I took the appointment. This time, I would put it in my calendar. Strike three.

And you know what is the worst about all of this was? Not one apology from anyone. Not even a phoned in apology with a sarcastic undertone. Instead, I was made to feel like it was my error. You're right, my fault. I shouldn't have gotten cancer.

Chapter 51

Thanks for Letting Me Know My Hair Is Growing Back

I've already mentioned that my hair was growing back. This was not a surprise; I didn't think I would remain bald forever. What was a surprise, was how surprised other people seemed to be about it.

I can't figure out why it irritated me so much when people saw sprouts of hair coming from my scarf and commented about how it was growing back. The next question was inevitably, "When are you gonna get rid of the scarf?" I mean, when toilet training a three-year-old, you don't get rid of the diaper just because she was able to use the potty successfully one time. She's not ready yet. I'm not ready yet. I'm not ready until the hair underneath my scarf looks better than my scarf.

The same scarf that I looked at with dread before I lost my hair, had become just as much a security blanket as my hair was before I lost it. Ripping it off for the first time was likely to produce the same level of anxiety as it did when I had to put it on for the first time. Strange how that happens. Just goes to show you that we are always looking for something to wrap ourselves in to shield us from the outside world. Or maybe that's just me.

The unveiling would be emotional as much as it will be liberating. I didn't know when it would happen, but I did know I didn't want to talk about it. Don't ask me about it. You will know I am ready to go without my scarf the day you see me going without my scarf.

Perspective is an interesting thing. When I first started wearing a scarf, I was sure people were looking at me with great sympathy. I was sure I would stand out like a sore thumb. While I did stand out, I noticed that my presence was really not my own. I became a walking memory for those who have been affected by cancer or know someone who has.

There was this restaurant in downtown Birmingham that Joe and I would go to every Wednesday. On one particular Wednesday, the waiter, an older gentleman, asked if he could buy me a glass of wine. I'm never turning down a free glass of wine, but I was curious as to why he would make such an offer. He touched my arm and said, "I want to buy you a glass of wine out of respect." Then he quickly walked away, leaving me no room to question.

At the end of the dinner, he came over to give us our bill. At this time, I was able to properly thank him. He said, "I hope you don't mind that I made an assumption that your scarf symbolizes cancer." I told him that he assumed correctly. He went on to tell me that so many people he cares about have been affected by cancer, and even two of the employees of the restaurant were currently dealing with it. He told me that those of us who have this cross to bear have been some of the most courageous and dignified people he had known. He explained how he had seen firsthand what such a diagnosis can do to a person's mind, body, and spirit, and yet here I was, enjoying a glass of wine.

Through my journey, I noticed the kindness of strangers emerge in ways I never imagined. This cancer experience has humbled me far beyond measure. But this man made me realize that I have had it wrong all along. People were not looking at me as someone to pity; they were looking at me as someone to admire.

While in my own world, I have had moments where I was crumbling so fast I didn't think the pieces would ever come together again. To the outside world, I was someone who symbolized strength, courage, and dignity.

That dinner was a moment of clarity for me. This man changed my narrative. I had emerged from a frail, scared woman, sure that people were looking at me with pity, to a badass motherfucker.

Chapter 52

The Day My Scarf Came off

In May, the school I worked at had a U Matter week. It is a week designed to help students understand that they are not alone. The week is made up of self-confidence building exercises. Among the events are the TEDx talks.

When I heard that students were looking for staff to speak at this event, I immediately volunteered. I have always loved public speaking, so whenever an opportunity arises, I jump on it.

The only stipulation was that our talk was about something significant in our lives. Naturally, I decided to talk about my journey through cancer. Writing my speech proved more cathartic and enlightening than I had imagined.

We so often go through life without much thought. Chronicling my journey throughout the year and then funneling it into a 20-minute presentation made me really look at the most poignant parts about my experience.

I talked about who I was before my diagnosis, and what my hair meant to me. How I dealt with losing it, and all of the people who came out of the woodwork to encourage me. Because of cancer, I reconnected with childhood and college friends. I formed relationships with the most unlikely people. Not because I had cancer, but because I had fear, and I wasn't afraid to talk about it. Because fear is a universal emotion, and because I created a safe place for people to talk about their fears, what happened was that they did. Human connection is the greatest connection anyone can have.

I had my speech written five weeks before I was scheduled to give it. I practiced it incessantly. I wanted to have every part memorized. I created slides of Jacob shaving my head, the chemo chair, and visuals that would help the audience come along with me on this journey for 20 minutes.

May 10th arrived, and I was scheduled to give my speech in front of a full auditorium. I was scheduled to go first. This was both terrifying and a relief. I realized my speech would set the tone for what would be the expectation for the rest of the day. At the same time, I would be able to listen to other presenters without the annoyance of going over my speech on repeat until it was my turn.

About three days before the event, I decided that this might be the perfect time for me to unveil my scarf. After all, my speech was all about vulnerability and stepping outside our comfort zones. To me, it would not be as impactful if I didn't practice what I preached. Also, if I ripped it off in front of everyone at the same time, I could avoid individual surprise.

As I was on the stage wrapping up my presentation, my nerves were at level 100. It was a do or die moment. If you listen to the presentation, you can see where my speech starts to slow at the very last moment. You can sense the hesitation.

But I did it. I took it off and was greeted by a surprising standing ovation. What I thought would be a moment of insurmountable vulnerability and exposure, turned into a moment of humbleness and empowerment.

Sometimes the things that weigh the most are the very things that set us free.

Chapter 53

And That's a Wrap

On May 30, 2017, I had my first cancer treatment. On May 30, 2018, I had my last. I don't know if I can adequately describe what it is like to go through such a visible, invasive illness. I hope that this book was able to give you a little insight.

I realize that I am one of the lucky ones. I will never say that I am lucky because no one who gets cancer is lucky. However, there are people who do not survive this. There are people whose side effects and treatments are so much more intense than mine.

But many of the emotions I went through are universal to all cancer patients. I hope that by bringing my story to you, it has allowed you to have a deeper understanding of what someone with cancer goes through.

Conclusion

I have learned that nothing is a given with cancer, and just because you feel good one day, does not mean you will feel good the next. I am learning to live in the moment and take the good days when they come. Today might be a good day. Tomorrow might suck ass. I have found this same thing to be true of life.

My hair grew back, but it was not the same hair that left. It doesn't have the same meaning that I once put on it. It no longer defines me. The hair on my head now tells a deeper, more meaningful story than the hair that left. It is more beautiful because it fought to get here. It will be stronger than what it left behind.

We all carry around our elephants. All of this time, I thought cancer was the elephant in the room. But it was really my hair. My hair, the importance I put on it, and its ability to act as a wall for which I could hide behind was the three-ton elephant that prevented me from looking deeper inside myself. It stopped me from noticing that I might have something to offer besides what I look like.

My elephants are smaller now. Being forced into a reality that makes you feel vulnerable all the time can make you stronger or weaker. For me, what it did was make me stand up and take notice. It made me lean in. It made me explore those parts of me that I would never have had the courage to do otherwise.

Instead of running from discomfort, now I name my demons so they can no longer have power over me. I talk about my fear so that it loosens its grip. I took up writing again; I wrote this book. I started a blog and podcast about anxiety and overcoming obstacles that prevent us from living our most inspired life. I don't know if I would have done any of these things had I not allowed myself to look deeper into who I was to find who I wanted to be.

This experience has taught me to challenge myself. It taught me to step outside of my comfort zone so I can be better. Someone once said that a comfort zone is a beautiful place, but nothing ever grows there. I could not agree with this more.

Life is not much different than jumping out of an airplane. It's scary at first; you have to take a leap of faith and free fall for a while, but if you pull the string, you will find that your shoot opens. If you allow yourself to open your eyes, what you will find is that the scenery is beautiful.

I don't believe that everything happens for a reason. I believe that things sometimes just happen, and it is our job to create the reason. My challenge to you is to embrace your moments, define them in a way that empowers you, and when you're standing at the edge of your airplane...Jump.

Noteworthy Suggestions If You Are About to Go Through Cancer Treatment

If you are reading this and about to embark on cancer treatments first, let me say that you are strong enough. You can do this. It will not be fun. It will not be easy. You will cry, you will be angry, you will be tired, you will be sick, you will feel out of control, you will feel like a science experience. Below are some suggestions that worked for me to make the road a little more controllable.

1. Find a support system. This is the single most important thing to have when going through all the shit you are about to go through. I feel extremely fortunate that I have such a wonderful group of friends and such supportive family around me. I couldn't have done any of this with any amount of courage if not for every one of them.

2. If you are going to lose your hair, don't let other people tell you when you should go bald. Hair is personal. What worked for one person may not work for you. For me, I wasn't interested in losing my hair before I lost my hair, so I waited for it to fall out in chunks. Some people say this causes more trauma. It didn't for me. In fact, because it was looking so gross toward the end, it was actually less traumatic for me to get rid of it entirely at that point.

3. If you don't want a wig, don't get a wig. If you want one, get one. End of story.

4. Silk scarves are difficult. They are so pretty, but they are slippery. Remember, your head is going to be flat. Like, F-L-A-T! Silk offers no dimension and no forgiveness. Whatever shape your head is will only be accentuated with a silk scarf. I opted for plain old bandannas or neck scarfs.

5. There are many ways to tie a scarf. I never adequately learned any. What I ended up doing was using a hair tie. Simply gather the base of the scarf at your neck (I gathered off to the side so that it gave the illusion of a side bun), loop a hair tie around twice (don't ever pull the ends of the scarf all the way through the hair tie) and shape the ends until it looks like a bun. You can leave the ends of the scarf to hang or wrap them back into your hair tie to secure. Sometimes I put a pretty flower clip on the bun portion of the scarf. This allowed for some flare.

6. Hats can look cute, but they look better if you get ones that come down over your ears. If you go to Amazon and type in "chemo hats," you will find there are a lot of options.

7. Winter is a great hiding place because you can just wear a winter hat along with the rest of the population. Everyone wears a hat, and many women with short hair look like they have no hair when they are wearing their winter hat. So for a brief moment in public, you are just you again—not the cancer girl.

8. Use an eyebrow pencil. I never fully lost my brows, but they got thinner and lighter. A bald head with no eyebrows is not a good look. You don't need to get expensive brands. I used e.l.f. Brow Pencil. It cost me $3.

9. Use non-waterproof mascara. Because lashes become thinner and more fragile, you need something not as harsh.

10. Now is the time to go bold with lipstick. I love my reds, pinks, and fuchsias. When you have no hair on your head, it draws attention to your face. Play up your features.

11. Use good lotion for face and body. Skin tends to get dry. I never found any one brand works better than another, but you might.

12. Carry Chap Stick everywhere. You will always need it.

13. Water sucks. I got to the point where I hated water. HATED IT! This might be because everything tasted like metal. I gotta be honest, I have no good suggestions. I tried everything. The best thing for me was to get Gatorade (you need the electrolytes when you have digestive issues) and put a little bit into my water. That way, I was drinking mostly water with a little flavor. I also really like chocolate coconut water. After chemo, your taste buds will be restored and water will taste like water again.

14. Diarrhea was the worst part for me. Carry a lot of Imodium. If you can, ask the doctor for a prescription. I also found that putting a heating pad on my stomach at night cut down on the cramping. I didn't have much nausea, but when I did, sucking on a peppermint and eating saltines helped.

15. The fatigue hits hard at times. It is important to give in to it when you can. I found that short 20-minute naps throughout the day helped.

16. You won't feel bad all the time. When you feel good, take advantage of it. Go out for drinks, hang out with friends. These times are limited and so

become more precious. You will find that your times of feeling good will become predictable, which makes it easier to plan. My worst days were days 3-8 after chemo treatment. But on day 14 or so, I felt almost normal.

17. Cry when you need to and don't apologize for it. This should be a general rule for everyone.

18. Get used to everyone knowing who you are but having no idea who they are. When you have a scarf on your head, you are easily identifiable. People will start conversations with you as if you are long lost friends. You will feel really stupid at first because you will think that your chemo brain has prevented you from remembering this friend. Then you will realize that they know you because you have cancer, and cancer prevents anonymity.

19. There will come a time when you do not wear your scarf (or wig) like a scarlet letter. There will even be times when you forget you have it on. These times will be obvious because you will see someone staring, and you will have the urge to ask them what the hell they are staring at. It is in those moments that you will feel a little bit of peace because you know you have come a long way.

20. If you want to rock out the bald head, do it!

21. Chemo brain is real. I always say that I have become stupid. At first, you might feel like you are getting dementia. You are not. I have forgotten events and names of household items; my ability to string a coherent sentence together became a challenge. This goes away in time.

22. You are going through grief. You have lost a part of who you are. You will go through all the stages of grief. This is normal. Some stages will last a day; others will last for the duration. Allow yourself to go through the feelings when they arise. At some point, you will get to acceptance. I promise.

23. Depending on the type of cancer you have, you may be thrown into medically induced menopause. This is where the Tamoxifen comes in. The hot flashes are HORRIBLE. Tamoxifen helps keep you in menopause, but for me, it also caused me to become extremely angry and depressed. My doctor supplemented it with an antidepressant, and this helped tremendously. It also cut down on the hot flashes.

Notable Suggestions for Family and Friends

If you are a friend or family member who just got the news that someone you love has been diagnosed with cancer, you likely feel helpless. It is human nature to want to be useful and helpful. We hate to see those we care about suffering, and it's hard accepting there is nothing you can do about it. Below are some things I suggest you do and don't do. There is no scientific data to back my findings. These are merely my opinion.

1. Please do not tell us how you know someone with cancer. This normalizes the experience and makes us feel like we cannot be upset that we have cancer.

2. If you have experienced cancer, tread lightly. This diagnosis is new to us and we are processing it. While we may want your advice at some point in our journey, we do not want it right away. We want our own experience.

3. Accept that there is nothing that you can do. We love you and know that you want to help. But offering advice, suggestions, research, or alternative treatment options will only make us feel angry.

4. A food train is usually a go-to way to help. Please keep in mind that we appreciate you feeding our family, but our taste buds are all messed up, and we likely do not want to eat anything.

5. Avoid giving us any carbonated beverage. This feels like glass shards going down our throats.

6. It doesn't have to be serious all the time. Keeping the humor is important. Those around me who appreciated how much I needed humor while I was going through this were lifesavers to me.

7. If you do want to help, here are some things that you can do:

a) If we have young children, take them for a day. Take them away from our house so we are not tempted to intervene. Guilt is strong when you are a parent.

b) Clean our house or hire a cleaning service.

c) Give us a journal. Writing is a very therapeutic way to manage feelings.

d) Just come sit with us. Don't plan on staying long; we get tired really easily. But your company is appreciated.

e) Garden. I have a wonderful community of people who actually built me an oasis. But I also had friends and family come over and just do yard work. This was extremely helpful.

Thank You

It's funny the stories we tell ourselves about who we are. When our story and our reality don't match, we tend to become anxious, or at least I do. For 43 years, I had been telling myself that if I walked into a room, surely no one would want to talk to me. If there was a game that requires picking teammates, I will always be the last one picked. When I did get a compliment, I assumed that I must have misrepresented myself. I have always been afraid to walk up to a group of people talking because I assumed that they will not want me there. The fear of getting found out has been my greatest fear.

So to have so many people come out of nowhere to support me was overwhelming. These people must not know who I am. I am a snarky, sarcastic, cynical person most of the time. The parts of me that I keep hidden are the parts that make me vulnerable, and for me vulnerability is the most uncomfortable feeling in the world. But I have shed more tears, and have been more humbled by the kindness of those around me than I knew what to do with. From a friend and her mother planting flowers in my front yard while I was at chemo, to Joe and his mother gardening, to a group of neighbors creating a gardening oasis (wait a minute...I see a theme). Work friends who have become real life friends gathering to support me for a Sunday brunch. Gift baskets, cards, meals, texts just to check up, friends and family who have come by just to sit with me. I felt guilty. Strange, right? I did though. I felt like I was hijacking people's time. I am in constant disbelief that anyone would want to do anything for me. There is a therapist somewhere waiting to get their hands on me.

I've told myself this story about who I am for so long that it has become like a security blanket to me. I felt anxiety thinking that anyone would want to take the time to help me, because the story that I have told myself along the way is that I am not worth helping. But what I am finding is that the one emotion that is the most terrifying to me, vulnerability, is the same one that ties us all together.

Vulnerability breeds human connection, and isn't life about connecting with people and getting to know their stories? I once heard that if you took the time to listen to someone else's story, you would never meet a person you didn't like. Something to keep in mind when you are talking to an asshole.

I will never be able to repay or properly thank all of the kindness that has been bestowed upon me. But one thing I do know is that these friends, coworkers, neighbors and family have written into my book a new chapter. And with that, perhaps I will begin to re-tell my story.

Below are the names of those who have impacted me. They are in no particular order. The worst part about thanking people is that I will inevitably leave someone out. But please know I appreciate everything that you have done for me. You have made a dent in my life, and have been a significant part of my experience.

My husband, Joe: Without you, I don't know how I would have made it through. Your unyielding support, patience, humor, and encouragement got me through the darkest days. Thank you for going to every single doctor's appointment with me. For sitting by my side in a really uncomfortable chair while I slept through six hours of chemotherapy. For filling the gaps when I was unable to function. I love you.

My son, Jacob: You were 8 years old when I had to tell you I had cancer. You handled it like a champ. You have had to deal with far more than is fair for such a young child. You are the light of my life. "You're my favorite."

To my Mom and dad, Dianne and Lenny: Thank you for your humor and willingness to jump in whenever I needed without question. Thank you for helping with the medical bills that cancer brings. You relieved so much stress. I love you.

My mother-in-law, Alice: I can never say enough about how much I appreciate everything you have done. From cleaning the house, to planting flowers, to doing my laundry, to just calling to check up. You have always made me feel so special and cared for. I love you.

My father-in-law, Derryl: I will never forget the few times we had the opportunity to eat lunch together, just the two of us. You were full of wisdom and are a man of integrity. They say that when you leave someone, you should hope that they are better for having known you. I am a better person because of what you brought to my life. Thank you for allowing me to be part of yours for 20 years. Your death was too soon, and you are greatly missed. I love you.

My sister, Jennifer: You have the perfect mix of humor and support. You always checked in on me, sent me flowers and words of support. You always know how to keep it light without demeaning the experience. Without your sarcasm, I am not sure I would have survived. Thank you for your support. I love you.

To my wine night ladies: Katie, Kelly, Melissa. Without you, I may never have gotten a mammogram. You continue to be a lifeline to me. Wine nights really do save lives. And to Scott, you shaved your head as I lost mine. You have all become family to me.

Lisa: Thank you for supporting me in the writing of this book. Only few are lucky enough to carry their childhood friends into adulthood. I am one of those lucky ones.

Lezah: Thank you for allowing me to cry, vent and just be present, without judgement. You have been a constant support all of our years of friendship and I don't think I can ever fully repay you or express how much you mean to me.

To all of Westacres: My community of Westacres is made up of the some of the most giving, empathetic, kind people. You delivered meals to me, tending my garden, built me an oasis in my backyard, complete with furniture, fountain and lights. I can never thank you enough. You are all a part of who I am, and will forever be etched in my story. I would be remiss if I did not mention a few of you by name. Please know that if I left you out, it is not because I do not appreciate you. It is because cancer has sucked out some brain cells.